JELLY ROLL™

QUILTS & MORE

Kimberly Einmo

American Quilter's Society
P. O. Box 3290 • Paducah, KY 42002-3290
www.AmericanQuilter.com

Located in Paducah, Kentucky, the American Quilter's Society (AQS) is dedicated to promoting the accomplishments of today's quilters. Through its publications and events, AQS strives to honor today's quiltmakers and their work and to inspire future creativity and innovation in quiltmaking.

Executive Book Editor: Andi Milam Reynolds
Senior Editor: Linda Baxter Lasco
Graphic Design: Lynda Smith
Cover Design: Michael Buckingham
Quilt Photography: Charles R. Lynch
How-to Photography: Kimberly Einmo
Additional Photography: Charlie Badalati

Additional copies of this book may be ordered from the American Quilter's Society, PO Box 3290, Paducah, KY 42002-3290, or online at www.AmericanQuilter.com.

Library of Congress Cataloging-in-Publication Data

Einmo, Kimberly.
  Jelly roll quilts & more / by Kimberly Einmo.
    p. cm.
  ISBN 978-1-57432-652-9   *4263 8600 3/10*
  1. Quilting--Patterns. 2. Patchwork--Patterns. I. Title.
  TT835.E447 2010
  746.46'041--dc22
                          2009042666

American Quilter's Society
P. O. Box 3290 • Paducah, KY 42002-3290
www.AmericanQuilter.com

Dedication

Dedicated with love and all the joy in my heart to my loving husband, Kent, and our darling boys, Joshua and Andrew. You are the light of my life and the reason I spend my days smiling and counting my blessings!

I'm very blessed to have had the love, support, and encouragement from my parents, Bill and Nina Wallace, from the time I was small. They planted the seeds of creativity that flourish in me today.

Thank you for your support, encouragement, laughter, and love. God bless you all.

Kimberly's Creed:

I love life—everything it has to offer and the endless possibilities of each new day.

I especially love to quilt and to share my passion and enthusiasm for quilting with everyone!

Fun Fact! Kent and I were both previously employed by the world's most famous mouse in Orlando, Florida. Not at the same time, however.

Acknowledgments

You may have heard that it "takes a village" to raise a child. In my case, it took a group of extremely talented quilters and friends to make this book possible.

Although mere words seem entirely inadequate, I wish to sincerely thank my true blue (or at least a lovely shade of periwinkle) friends for lending their time and amazing talents to help create the quilts and road test the patterns for many of the projects in this book. Without their help, encouragement, enthusiasm, and support, this book would not have come together in the way it did and my life would not be the exuberant rainbow of colors it is without their presence and steadfast friendship.

Thank you, ladies, for sharing your creativity, sense of humor, and candor and for stepping up to the challenge of making these projects while they were in the "testing" stage. You are each a genuine blessing in my life. I am eternally grateful!

Carolyn Archer	Roseanne Mamer
Ilona Baumhofer	Claire Neal
Carla Conner	Judy Schrader
Miriam Fay	Birgit Schüller
Jan Hossenlopp	Cindy Siefferlen

I'd especially like to thank Lissa Alexander and all the good folks at Moda Fabrics and United Notions for their generous support and for supplying the sumptuous fabrics used to make the quilts in this book.

And my sincere thanks go to the very talented gentleman behind the camera for the photos of the Jelly Roll retreat, Charlie Badalati. His gift for viewing the world through a camera lens is a gift to us all.

I'd also like to sincerely thank my publisher, Meredith Schroeder; my editors, Linda Lasco and Andi Reynolds; graphic designer, Lynda Smith; and all the extremely creative folks at the American Quilter's Society for their ability to capture so beautifully the vision I had in my mind's eye for this book. You all have treated me like part of the team since we collaborated on my first book, *Quilt a Travel Souvenir*. I'm blessed beyond measure to be associated with such an amazing group of exceptional people!

Table of Contents

Preface

It's not your grandmother's quilting anymore. Heck, in today's world it's not even your mom's quilting anymore; not by a long shot.

Today's quilter is savvy; she's smart, hip, likes fresh new ideas, has a wide variety of interests, and juggles a career, her family, and friends. And she does it with style, flair, and fabric!

Today's quilter is enthusiastic and like a sponge for soaking up the latest in techniques and quilting know-how. She may have a limited budget, but she is clever, creative, and knows the best, most economical places to find top-quality fabric and notions. She is thrifty!

Today's quilter may also have life experience. Perhaps lots of it! She has raised her family, paved her way through the working world, and now has time to devote to leisure, to her passion, her friends, travel, and adventure.

Today's quilter wants to do it all. She is busy! This is the reason why she is always on the lookout for fresh new ideas, colors, current trends and patterns which are easy, fun, and fabulous.

Today's quilter may be a man!

Yes, I'm talking to YOU! As a quilter in today's hectic world, you don't have time to spend fussing with old-fashioned, outdated techniques. Your quilting time is precious, and you love to use the latest and greatest tools and newest speed piecing and machine-appliqué techniques so you can actually complete your projects and enjoy them at home, in your office, or share them with special recipients.

There are many terrific new products available on the market designed to make quilting faster, easier, and more accurate, and today's quilter loves to experiment and try new things. Today's quilter is eager to embrace advances in technology, has become computer literate, and surfs the Internet to her (or his!) advantage.

With all the advances in technology in the quilting world, the fabric manufacturers jumped on board and worked hard to "reinvent the wheel," introducing all sorts of new and different precut fabric packs that appeal to today's quilter. These laser precision-cut bundles of calorie-free sweetness are irresistible for so many reasons. They are a fabulous way to sample every piece of fabric from a particular line and the quilts made from them are scrappy yet beautifully and effortlessly balanced and color coordinated.

As a quilter in this modern world you need versatile and fabulous quilting patterns you can easily adapt to incorporate your own creative design ideas, and to truly utilize your sewing machine's capabilities to bring those ideas to life! You need ideas to organize and improve your quilting space and lots of useful hints and tricks to make your piecing more accurate and efficient. You also need a few tried-and-true favorite recipes to make the most of your busy lifestyle to maximize your quilting time. And if you are entertained along the way, well, that's just icing on the cake! (Ahem, a Layer Cake that is.)

You are the present and future of the quilting world. You are the new, millennium quilter of tomorrow.

Today's quilter is YOU!

Introduction

Let me say right up front this isn't just an ordinary book of quilt patterns. This book is different. There. I've said it. Big words and a bold promise. So, what's different, you ask? You already know the basic idea behind this book because you've seen the cover and you've read the title. (The secret's out....)

This book is different because I've written it in the first person as if I'm talking directly to you. I want to be your personal quilt coach. I'm the teacher who is available, at your beck and call 24 hours a day; always there for you whenever you feel like cutting or stitching. And this book is like your personal quilt class with one-on-one instruction. Even late at night when you're in your jammies. Or on that cold, drizzly day when you play hooky from work and stay home to sew. Every time you pick up this book and open the pages, you'll find I have insights to share, tips and techniques to teach you, new challenges to help you stretch your creative muscles, and even some of my very favorite tasty treats for you to try. (Yep, there's a little bit of Paula Deen in me, too!)

I've designed this book to help you not only make the most of every moment you have to quilt, but to have fun while you're doing it! The projects in this book are also different from what you've seen before. The quilts may look complex but they are designed with you in mind. They are fast yet fabulous. The instructions and illustrations are clear and easy to understand. And best of all, you get to make quilts with all those wonderful new pre-cut fabric packs or strips and scraps from your own stash. How great is that?

I've always been a hands-on, ever-encouraging, always engaging type of instructor. I love introducing students to new and different things and witnessing those Oprah "ah-ha!" moments when the light goes on and they understand and really "get it." So I've written this book to help you discover your own ah-ha quilting moments. All I ask is that you're open minded and willing to try a new thing or two....or three. Or four. Don't be afraid to step out of your personal quilting comfort zone and try something new and different. You'll not only learn and grow but you'll have fun along the way. I promise!

As with my first book, *Quilt a Travel Souvenir*, at the end of each project chapter there is a special Try This! section with some of my very favorite quick and clever hints, tips, and even a few recipes sprinkled throughout to encourage you to try something new-to-you. You'll never know what you can learn or accomplish unless you try. Each Try This! exercise or recipe is quick, easy, delicious, informative, or fun so you'll have that great feeling that comes from learning something new along the way!

As your personal quilting coach, I'll be with you every step of the way. If you have a question, need an idea or two, or just want to share photos of your beautiful quilts (which I would absolutely love to see), let me hear from you. It's just another way for me to be in touch so you can state with confidence and pride that you have your own personal quilting guru. (Doesn't that have a nice ring to it?) You can always contact me through my Web site at: www.kimberlyeinmo.com, or send me an e-mail at Kimberly@kimberlyeinmo.com.

Now, enough said. Let's get ready to Try This! and make some fabulous quilts!

Chapter One

Get Ready...

Take a moment to READ THIS to get to all the good stuff that's coming!

I won't spend a lot of time or space in this book going over all the basics of quiltmaking because let's face it—you didn't buy this book to learn basic quiltmaking. You bought this book because you want to make some (or all!) of the gorgeous quilts from Jelly Rolls and precut fabric packs featured inside. So if you're a brand new quilter, my advice would be to take a basic quilting class from a knowledgeable instructor or partner with an experienced quilting buddy, pick her brain, and learn her techniques to expand your skills and become as proficient as you can.

In the meantime, however, read through this section and get ready to dive right in and have some FUN! Yes, even beginners can tackle these projects. The quilts are quick and easy, fast and fabulous, and you'll feel instant gratification while using precut fabric bundles.

What you'll need:
fabrics, tools, and basic supplies

A room with a view....or not

Whether you have a tiny closet or a spacious, custom sewing studio, you'll need to have some space to work. By all means, don't be discouraged if you only have a little room or even if you're sharing your space with other family members (like the kitchen table or family room.) But do carve out a niche for yourself and make it your own even if you have to put things away at meal time or tidy up stray pins for the kids to do their homework. If you have a guest room or even a corner in the basement or attic, use the space that is available and make it comfortable. If you have a room with windows and good natural light,

consider it a bonus. But if the only sewing space you have is a room without windows, don't sweat the small stuff. One of my favorite sewing areas was a cozy basement room without any windows and I made it work with bright lighting, a few green plants scattered around, and great tunes playing on my CD player. The point is, I made do with what I had available to me at the time and called it my own.

Back it up

A good chair with proper back support is essential. One that adjusts its height so you don't have to reach up or strain to reach the bed of your sewing machine is best. Your arms should be perpendicular to your body when sitting at your sewing machine. If your chair doesn't reach high enough, try using a firm pillow to boost your body. The more comfortably you are seated, the longer you'll be able to sew without muscle fatigue, a sore back, or stiff neck.

Let there be light!

Good lighting is essential. If you are working in a poorly lit area, your eyes will be strained and it won't be long before you'll develop headaches and a host of other complaints. You'll also lose accuracy when you sew and your stitching lines won't be straight and even. Who wants their seams to look like a dog's hind leg? Besides, you won't be able to see your fabrics and all the colors and hues properly, and that's certainly no fun. Invest in one or more of the full-spectrum lights or light bulbs and save your sight. Trust me when I tell you your vision begins to go after 40 anyway. So why rush the process or make it worse?

Your all-time favorite appliance

If it isn't already, I'll bet your sewing machine will soon become your favorite plug-in appliance. My sewing machines are my mechanical best friends and I treat them as such. Your sewing machine needs to be in good working condition to make the quilts in this book. So let me ask you, when was the last time you had your sewing machine serviced? Ah ha! Can't remember? Well then, it's time!

A sewing machine should be serviced by an authorized dealer at least once a year—perhaps even more frequently if you put a hundred thousand miles on it in a matter of months. When you take it to be serviced, consider it like taking your MBF (mechanical best friend) in for a spa treatment. You can use the time it's at the spa to prepare your sewing area and do all your cutting or any other preparations so when you pick up your machine you'll be ready for hours of stress-free, tension-free (neck muscle tension, that is) stitching. After a good tune-up, your machine will hum like it's brand new!

Kimberly's top tip:
Make an appointment to have your machine serviced while you're on vacation, or at the same time each year you have your mammogram. (You know you need to do this, ladies!) I take mine in on my birthday. It's one of the best birthday presents I can give to myself!

In between full-service tune-ups, you'll want to keep the moving parts free from lint. You will need to carefully clean the bobbin area with a lint brush, or better yet, use the tiny attachments made for vacuum cleaners to suck out any stray threads and lint build-up. Don't blow into the bobbin casing area to clean out the lint. The mechanical parts in your machine don't respond well to the moisture in your breath. You can use a can of compressed air, but try to angle the long, pointed nozzle so that the lint is blown out (from back to front) of the machine, not farther into the deeper recesses of the bobbin casing area.

Following your sewing machine's instruction manual, oil your machine if necessary. Can't find your owner's manual? Many sewing machine companies have instruction manuals online or available to download, or you can contact their customer service department with any questions you may have regarding general maintenance. I highly recommend you establish good rapport with your local sewing machine dealer. A good dealer is there to assist you in so many ways and is invaluable to help you troubleshoot so you're not left scratching your head with unanswered questions and nowhere to turn.

The bottom line is, make yourself happy with a fully functioning sewing machine. Nothing spoils the fun of quilting faster than a machine that keeps breaking down, has tension troubles, or continually gets clogged with thread. Last but not least, begin each project with a sharp new needle. (More on needles to come.)

Your sewing machine's best friends (besides you)

There are a few specialty presser feet you'll need to make the quilts in this book. If you don't have them already, contact your local dealer (another reason to have that great dealer rapport established) or search online to see if you can order them. At the very least, you'll need to know if your machine is a high-shank, low-shank, or a Singer® slant. Check the owner's manual if you're not sure.

Piecing Foot

Almost all sewing machine manufacturers now carry a special ¼" piecing foot for their machines. I can't begin to emphasize just how much this will change everything about your quilting life! In all of quilting, but most especially to make the quilts in this book, you will need to use a scant ¼" seam allowance. Some piecing feet even come with a fabric guide along the side to keep your seams from straying past the edge of the foot. It is wonderfully accurate and will make all the difference between a chunky ¼" seam and a perfect, scant ¼" seam! Once you have your piecing foot attached, make a test seam and measure the row of stitching from the edge of the fabric with a ruler. You may need to adjust your needle position by one or two threads to obtain that perfect scant ¼". Invest in one of these feet and never piece without it again. Ask me how I know!

Open-Toe Appliqué Foot

This foot may come in a variety of widths (for example, 6mm or 9mm) and usually has an open space or clear plastic between the toes of the foot so you can see the stitching area clearly. You'll need this foot to do an invisible appliqué stitch or a buttonhole stitch along the edges of your fused appliqué shapes. I find this foot helpful for attaching binding and doing decorative stitching as well.

Simple, fast, and easy, the fusible appliqué shapes in this book are a wonderful way for you to use all those sewing machine feet you have on hand for embellishing but rarely have a chance to use. Yep, it's time to take off the ¼" piecing foot (Can't remember the last time you did?) and try out those feet made especially for sewing on trims, rickrack, lace, and even pearls. If you don't have trims available, just use your built-in decorative stitches and some beautiful decorative threads. These days, anything goes (literally!) on quilts and it's all about the bling and embellishments. Step out of your comfort zone when it comes to embellishing your blocks and use those sewing machine feet, trims, and specialty threads!

Walking Foot

For straight-line machine quilting, you may need an attachment called a walking foot. This foot is also called an even-feed foot or plaid matcher. Some machines come equipped with a built-in dual feed mechanism, which works just like a walking foot. The walking foot allows two or more layers of fabric to be fed underneath the presser foot evenly so there are no pleats or puckers when you quilt the layers together. You will use this attachment or mechanism to quilt straight lines or very gentle curves.

Free-Motion Foot

For free-motion quilting you will need to use a free-motion or darning foot. The feed dogs on your sewing machine must be lowered to use this foot. Some machines come with an attachment to cover the feed dogs instead. Check your owner's manual or ask your dealer about your particular model of sewing machine. With the feed dogs disengaged, you will have complete control over the speed and direction in which you move the quilt as the needle moves up and down. You may need to adjust the top thread or bobbin tension to achieve just the right tension for free-motion quilting. This will take some practice, so be sure to use a sample quilt "sandwich" (top fabric, batting, and backing fabric layered together) before you actually try free-motion quilting on your pretty quilt top. Don't be intimidated by experimenting with the tension settings. There is nothing you can do that can't be undone.

Kimberly's top tip:
Free-motion quilting takes patience and practice. Even the most experienced quilters had big, clunky stitches at first. Prepare a sample quilt sandwich about 18" square. This is enough fabric to move freely underneath the needle but not so large as to impede your movements.

As your personal quilt coach, I want you to keep your shoulders down (don't let them inch up around your ears) and keep breathing. Whenever I teach free-motion quilting in class, so many students initially end up holding their breath! You don't want the speed of the machine to be too slow, but don't feel pressure to push the pedal to the metal, either. Find your own personal rhythm and the speed that works best for you.

Practice without distractions and always be mindful of the position of your fingers. If your machine has a needle down option, this is helpful when you need to stop and readjust your hands or the position of the quilt sandwich. Practice a simple, random pattern of gentle curves and loops on a sample quilt sandwich. As you relax and your stitches become smoother, try writing your name or making small hearts or flower designs. Most importantly, have fun experimenting and feel empowered!

Give yourself permission....

If all else fails—you just can't get the hang of free-motion machine quilting, you're feeling guilty or frustrated, and you're ready to move on to piecing another project in this book—contact a local longarm machine quilter and take your beautifully pieced top to her. As soon as you're out the door to deliver it, you can consider it done (no more UFOs!) and you'll be ready to move on to the next quilt top. There is nothing wrong with this option, and you can piece to your heart's content without any guilt. Consider that you're doing your part to help a small business keep its doors open in this tough economy!

Straight to the point: Needles

I've already asked you a tough question about the last time you took your machine to a dealer for regular maintenance and service. Now let me ask you, when was the last time you changed the needle in your sewing machine? Can't remember? What's that you say? You can't even tell me what kind of needle is currently in your machine? My goodness, don't tell the quilt police! But it doesn't matter because you're making a fresh start from this point forward anyway. Let's discuss.

The basic rule of thumb is this: you should throw away your used needle for every eight hours of continuous use. If you can't remember when you changed it last, change it. And don't just change it, throw the old needle out. If you are doing machine embroidery, change your needle even more frequently since it will wear out much faster than when doing regular sewing. Don't wait until a needle breaks to change it. And if you're sewing and your machine is making an odd, clunking sound, one of the first things you should do to troubleshoot is to change your needle. If a needle is dull or has a burr on the shank, it will make a strange or popping noise as it pierces the fabric.

There are many different kinds of sewing machine needles for a wide variety of uses. Use a needle specifically made for the type of thread and fabric you are stitching. For the types of projects in this book, you'll want to use a size 80 sharp or quilting needle. Take some time to do a little research and ask questions at your local quilt shop. Stock up on a variety of needles and keep them handy. Adopt one of my good habits: I like to treat myself to a new pack of quilting needles every time I shop at my local quilt shop. Needles are staples (like canned goods) and don't have an expiration date, so they don't go bad, and you'll always have the right type or size ready to go at a moment's notice.

Kimberly's top tip:
It can be dangerous to throw away used needles and straight pins into the trash, so keep an empty dental floss or mints box handy for discarding needles and pins. Wait until it is filled before throwing the closed container in the trash.

Pressing matters: Your iron and ironing board

A high-quality iron with steam capabilities is essential. Make sure the sole plate is clean. If it is dirty or has sticky residue on it from previous projects, take the time to clean it with a cleaner made just for sole plates. If you are in the position to purchase a new iron, shop for one that will produce lots of steam. You might even consider buying an iron with a separate water tank. Its constant steam and consistent high heat are invaluable. Another feature to consider when purchasing a new iron is one without automatic shut-off.

As quilters, we might not use our iron at regular intervals, so it can be frustrating to pick up your iron to press a seam and find it is already cool from having shut itself off. (But be sure to remember to turn it off yourself when you are finished!)

If your ironing board cover also has remnants of that sticky, fusible adhesive, wash the cover or invest in a new one. Your ironing board should be sturdy and placed close to your sewing machine at a comfortable height.

If you or someone you know is handy with wood, a saw, hammer, and nails, you might want to consider making a large pressing surface to cover the top of your ironing board. It's easy and inexpensive and the materials can be purchased at a hardware, lumberyard, or home building supply warehouse.

For instance, purchase a piece of 1" thick board and cut it to this size: 20" x 60" x 1". Use small pieces of wood and measure them to fit around the sides of your ironing board. Nail these "anchors" to the underside of the board. Cut equal-sized pieces of cotton batting; heat resistant, reflective silver fabric; and a layer of heavy broadcloth or ticking about eight inches larger than the top of the wood. Use a staple gun to secure all the layers to the underside of your big board. You now have a large surface to sit securely on top of your ironing board for pressing your pieced units, blocks, and yardage. Simply remove the board whenever you need to iron clothes.

A high fiber diet: Fabric

The quilts in this book were all made using 100% cotton fabric. Generally speaking, most quilts are made using all cotton fabric. However, you might be able to incorporate different fibers such as wool, silk, and rayon into your quilts depending on the project. Typically, you'll want to avoid polyester blends for your quilts. When buying cotton fabric, take care to purchase top-quality fabric and avoid bargain basement, poor quality cottons. The old saying, "You get what you pay for" never rings more true than when talking about quilting fabric. You're not sure what the fiber content is? Give it the burn test. Take a small swatch of your fiber and set it on fire in a safe, well-ventilated area. After it burns, if there are only ashes left behind, then it is 100% cotton or another natural fiber such as linen. If it melts or leaves a residue other than ash, it has synthetic material in it.

The ties that bind: Thread

For piecing: My preference is to use cotton thread for piecing cotton fabric. Silk-covered cotton thread is my personal favorite as there is less lint build-up in the bobbin casing area. As for color, I choose a neutral color that blends with the fabrics such as ecru, natural, or light gray. When working with a black background, I use black or charcoal gray thread. Your sewing machine may work best with one brand of thread rather than another. Ask your dealer for recommendations or try several different brands until you find the one that works best for you and your machine.

For quilting: There are many new, exciting threads in a wide variety of fiber content and weights (from very fine to extra heavy) available today. Different threads will give you different effects for quilting and embellishing so don't be afraid to try them. Just make sure you match the needle size and type to the thread you are using (such as a metallic needle with a metallic thread) and test on a sample quilt sandwich before sewing directly onto your quilt. Experiment and enjoy the results.

For appliqué: Generally, for machine appliqué I like to match the color of the thread I'm using to the color of the appliqué piece, not the background fabric. However, it can be fun and very dramatic to use a high-contrasting color of thread when using a buttonhole appliqué stitch. Black thread can pack a visual punch and look very retro, depending on the project. Monofilament (invisible) thread is essential when doing invisible machine appliqué stitching. You'll want to use cotton thread in the bobbin that matches your background fabric so if any of the bobbin threads pull through to the front they will blend in. Another favorite of mine is silk thread for machine appliqué and quilting. It can be a little pricey, but oh-so worth the extra cost for fabulous results.

Batting a thousand

While there are many wonderful battings available to choose from, I usually choose a batting with a cotton/poly blend and the thinnest loft possible. For wallhangings, I prefer my battings to drape beautifully, rather than have high loft or extra warmth. Recently, batting companies have been "going green" with wonderful new options such as battings made from bamboo, corn, and other organic materials. Test different varieties or ask for recommendations from your quilting friends to find out their personal favorites. Be sure to read and follow the manufacturer's directions for pre-shrinking if required.

The cutting edge: Rotary cutter and mat

If you thought I was a stickler when it comes to having your sewing machine serviced regularly and for changing the needle in your machine frequently, just wait until you hear what I have to say about the blade in your rotary cutter! There's almost nothing worse than a dull blade, so make yourself a promise to change to a new blade with every new quilt project, or whenever your blade gets a burr (a spot that always skips cutting in the same place). You won't believe how wonderful it is to cut multiple layers of fabric like a hot knife through butter!

Kimberly's top tip:
Recycle used rotary blades! Just because a blade isn't sharp enough to cut your fabric anymore doesn't mean it doesn't have a useful life left. Keep an extra rotary cutter handy just to cut paper, template plastic, art and school projects, wrapping paper, bubble wrap, batting, and opening boxes.

Storing used blades: Save those circular metal mint tins (think peppermint patties) and line it with a small piece of leftover batting. These tins make an ideal place to store all your used blades until you need them or until you have enough to throw away in the trash safely.

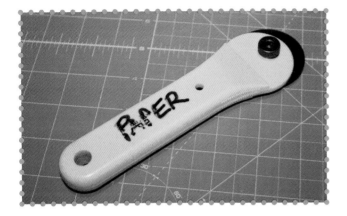

While a 45mm cutter is probably the most versatile of all the available sizes of rotary cutters to have on hand, it's a treat to have different size cutters for different uses. For instance, I use an 18mm cutter to cut basic appliqué shapes and a 60mm cutter for up to six layers of fabric at one time accurately. You may think having one rotary cutter is enough, but consider putting different size rotary cutters on your holiday wish list for a thoughtful elf to stuff your stocking. There are many different brands, so don't be shy—ask to "road test" different styles at your local quilt shop. Chances are they have several different brands available for use by the staff in their workroom, and you can test them to see which one is the best and most comfortable "fit" for your hand.

Always use a self-healing mat when cutting with a rotary cutter. The larger the mat, the easier it is to measure and cut large pieces of fabric accurately. Try using your kitchen counter or other flat surface that is higher than a standard table. The extra height will be kinder to your back and allow you to cut without pain for extended periods of time. Even a standard washer or dryer is typically the right height for you to cut without bending over

at an awkward angle. Take care and always store your mats flat so they don't warp. Never roll them or leave them in a hot car or in direct sunlight! Consider storing them under a bed when not in use if you don't have a dedicated cutting surface.

Scissors

You'll need a variety of types and sizes of scissors on hand, including a good, sharp pair of shears and small, sharp snips for cutting threads at the machine. Be sure to keep your fabric and paper scissors separate. Mark them with color-coded ribbons tied on to the handles if necessary so you don't dull your fabric scissors by cutting paper or template plastic. One of the best gifts you can give yourself is a pair of sharp scissors. A high quality pair will last a lifetime if treated properly. I take all my scissors to be sharpened every year during the week of my birthday. It's easy to remember to do this if you make it a yearly ritual, and it's a great birthday gift to yourself to have fresh, sharp shears!

Do you measure up? Acrylic rulers

Everyone who knows me knows I am a ruler fanatic. I like to collect, experiment with, and use a wide variety of rulers when I'm rotary cutting. In fact, I've actually invented four new rulers to date (my dad is so proud—I did something really productive with math!) and I'll explain more about those in the coming pages. But at the minimum, you'll need a 6½" x 24" ruler and a 15" x 15" square ruler to make the quilts in this book.

Get to the point! Marking tools

A good mechanical pencil is a necessity, and chalk wheels in a variety of colors are quite helpful for marking templates, appliqué shapes, and quilting lines. Tailor's chalk also works quite well and I have had good success with those white and blue pens with disappearing ink. However, test any marking tool to make sure the marks really disappear from your fabric before using them directly on your project.

Get Ready...

Straight pins

Straight pins are a must-have for piecing and quilting. The thinner the pins, the smaller the holes left in your fabric. If your pins are bent or rusted, throw them out and splurge on a new box. Better yet, get one of those magnetic pin cushions. They are amazing! If you drop any pins on the floor, all you have to do is wave your magnetic pin cushion about 4"–6" above the area and the pins will magically jump off the floor and onto the magnet without you having to pick each pin up individually. This is a great time-saver and prevents your tootsies from getting stuck. And be sure to keep straight pins stored away from tiny hands and furry friends as well. (For some reason, steel pins are like catnip to felines. Ask me how I know.)

Personally, I prefer the flat-head flower pins because they are extra long, slim, and nice to use when I'm pinning seams and matching points. You can even iron over them, but be careful not to machine stitch over any pins. Instead, pull each pin out just before the needle reaches them when sewing a seam.

Notion commotion: Seam ripper

As my mom used to say, "As you sew, so shall you rip!" Ripping out a seam is just a fact of quilting life; even the most advanced quilters have to rip now and then. I've witnessed students on many occasions working much too hard or damaging their fabrics simply because they were using an old, rusty, dull seam ripper or one with the sharp point broken off. Why struggle? Buy yourself a new seam ripper! They are very inexpensive and will make the task of ripping far less daunting. However, these little gems can be dangerous if the point and blade are left exposed, so be sure to put the cap back on when it is not in use.

Basting options

There are many ways to baste your quilt sandwich together, but my favorite basting method is to use one of those basting guns and a plastic grid (for underneath the layered quilt). Adhesive sprays are efficient, as are fusible battings. Size #1 curved safety pins are yet another way to baste your quilts and effectively hold your layers together. Try them all and choose your favorite method. Or better yet, train your significant other or have your kids help you for a little extra stipend in their allowance. Many hands make light work!

Stabilizers

I could write pages and pages about the benefits of stabilizers and the many different types that are available and how to use them. But for the purposes of this book, you'll only need a temporary—or tear-away—stabilizer to use underneath machine appliqué or decorative stitching. Tear-away stabilizers are available on a roll or folded in a package. Make sure you buy a temporary stabilizer. You don't want to use the permanent or cut-away stabilizer on any of these projects.

Fusible web

Paper-backed fusible web makes machine appliqué quick and easy. It is best to choose a light- or medium-weight fusible web if you are using 100% cotton fabric. Be sure to read the manufacturer's instructions and test the fusible on a scrap of fabric before using it for your project.

Kimberly's top tip:
Fusible web does not store well, so don't stock up when there's a sale if you don't plan to use it within six months. The web may become brittle or sticky over time. Buy just what you'll need to use. I speak from years of experience and yards and yards of unusable fusible because I was trying to be thrifty and "stock up."

Sewing essentials

Everyone needs to have a dedicated sewing basket, bucket, pouch, or even a rubber tub filled with some sewing essentials. These basic sewing supplies (BSS) include all of the things I've listed above plus a few other essential items such as a thimble, needle threader, bodkin, shish kabob skewer, small safety pins, fine-tip permanent ink marker or Pigma® pen, small ruler, seam gauge, measuring tape, a variety of hand sewing needles, and bee's wax. Have fun stocking up on these items when there is a sale at your local fabric store or make a wish list to keep on hand. Many of these items are very inexpensive and make great gifts for secret sisters or just for yourself—because you're worth it!

To wash or not to wash—that is the question!

This topic has been hotly debated for decades in the quilting world and there are two distinct camps on the subject: those who always prewash their fabrics before cutting and those who don't. I was always in the first camp and was diligent about prewashing every piece of fabric that came through my door before it was allowed to live in my stash or be cut up for a quilt. In recent years I've relaxed my personal policy for a number of reasons. To be sure, there will always be fabrics that should—no, MUST—be prewashed before being sewn into a quilt such as some batik fabrics and very saturated, dark colors such as red, blue, black, and any colors or fabrics prone to bleeding.

However, when working on the quilts for this book, I quickly learned that attempting to prewash the precuts was going to be futile and a huge waste of time. So, I relaxed my policy and dove right in with complete abandon to cut and sew without worrying about bleeding or shrinkage. And I'm a happier person for doing so. My advice to you—don't worry about prewashing your fabrics or precuts to make the quilts in this book. Give yourself permission to "just let it go" and have fun!

Neat vs. sloppy

I've said it before and I'll say it again…I'm a neat-nick! I truly believe in taking a bit of extra time to trim all the pointy dog ears from pieced units and stray threads from seams. If you trim your threads and unwanted fabric tabs as you go, the task of neatening up your blocks won't be so daunting and your seams will lie flat and even. So I'd like you to adopt the habit of being a neat-nick quilter like me, and you'll see dramatic improvements in all your piecing efforts. I promise!

Kimberly's best tip ever!

I like to use spray sizing when I iron freshly washed fabrics, and I use it on fabric strips and other precut units, too. Nothing takes out the wrinkles as nicely and makes your fabrics behave as well. Unlike spray starch, spray sizing is a synthetic so it won't be a food source to attract moths and silverfish. Spray sizing also makes your cut pieces cling together ever so slightly, and it helps to keep bias edges from stretching.

Chapter Two

Get Set...

How to use this book—it is as easy as 1 – 2 – 3!

I've gone over the basic quilting essentials, so I trust you did read Chapter One. And it was actually fun to read, right? Now I'll give you a brief overview of how to use this book. It's easy! Just follow a few simple directions and keep an open mind when it comes to stepping out of your comfort zone and trying some new-to-you techniques. You may have a favorite method for making half-square triangles, but take a few moments to try my method and compare. You'll learn some new things along the way—even if you're an experienced quilter—and you'll expand your skills while having fun. This is no-stress quilting at its best!

There are some abbreviations I use in the instructions (to save a little time and space):

HST	half-square triangle
RST	right sides together
WST	wrong sides together

First, let's discuss precuts. "What's a Jelly Roll?" I used to hear this question all the time but less frequently these days as just about everyone in the quilting world is now familiar with these wonderful, basic precut fabric strips. But if you're not familiar with these sweet little textile goodies, allow me to personally introduce them to you.

Jelly Rolls are my personal favorites of the precut bundles. Each Jelly Roll contains 40 different 2½" x 44" strips from a single line of fabric, all rolled up delectably and tied with a bow. They are fun to collect and a great bargain for your buck considering you get a wide selection of fabrics for a coordinated, scrappy effect without the work of having to gather 40 different fabrics and cutting a strip from each one!

Honey Buns arrived on the quilting scene more recently and are similar to Jelly Rolls except they contain 40 different 1½" x 44" strips from a single line of fabric. They are wonderful not only for making quilts and projects by themselves, but they are also perfect for pairing with other precut bundles to make an even wider variety of blocks and basic piecing units.

Layer Cakes are made up of 40 (some packs have 42!) different 10" x 10" squares from a single line of fabric. Oh, the many things you can do with a Layer Cake. You can cut squares, triangles, rectangles, and even a variety of appliqué shapes! They play ever-so-nicely with other precuts. This way we can have our cake (fat and calorie free!) and make quilts, too.

Charm Packs are simply 5" x 5" squares from a single line of fabric and contain anywhere from 25 to 40 squares, depending on the fabric line. They are perfect for so many uses and pair beautifully with Jelly Roll strips to make hundreds of basic blocks. Personally, I think they should be called Cupcakes since they are miniature versions of Layer Cakes. (I wonder if the powers-that-be at Moda have thought of this.)

Turnovers are triangles from 6" squares that have been cut in half, so they contain two of each fabric for a total of 80 triangles per package. These are cut perfectly with a 45-degree angle; no muss, no fuss.

Fat Quarter Packs are just what their name implies. They contain one fat quarter of every print in a particular line of fabric, all folded, stacked neatly, and tied with a bow. To be specific, each fat quarter is an 18" x 22" piece of fabric. It is literally a "fat" quarter yard instead of a skinny quarter yard, which measures 9" x 44."

These laser precision cut bundles of calorie-free sweetness are irresistible for so many reasons. They are a fabulous way to sample every piece of fabric from a particular line and the quilts made from them are fast, easy, and accurate! All the hard work of gathering coordinating prints and fabrics has been done for you, and all you need to do is some basic quick and easy cutting into the size units you need to create an unlimited number of scrappy quilts and projects. What's not to love?

Moda Fabrics was the first company to introduce these precut fabric bundles, but other fabric manufacturers have jumped on the quilt wagon and many now offer their own versions of these fabulous fabric line samples. Precut fabric bundles are readily available in most quilt shops and some discount fabric stores, and of course you'll find them in abundance on the Internet. Just use your favorite Internet search engine and you'll have more shopping choices than you can imagine!

Great for stash busting!

You don't *need* to have these precut bundles to make the quilts in this book. You can easily make your own precut bundles by simply cutting strips (or squares or triangles) from fabrics in your stash or ask your local quilt shop if they offer an accurate cutting service of fabrics of your own choosing bundled together. The quilts I've designed are natural stash busters and a great way to use up small leftover bits of fabric or even "ugly" fabrics you wouldn't use for quilts with a more planned look.

Use fabrics you already have on hand or even from your scrap basket by simply cutting your own strips or units according to the fabric requirements chart listed for each quilt. Why not consider organizing a strip swap with your quilting buddies or your local guild? For example, it would be easy to gather enough different fabric strips between you and four of your friends if each swap participant brought one strip of eight different fabrics for everyone in the swap.

My favorite methods to make the easiest, fastest, most accurate, basic quilting units ever!

If you can master these tried and true, speedy-yet-accurate techniques for making four-patch units, half-square triangles, and Flying Geese units, you can piece almost anything! In all of quilting, you'll see these three units over and over again. They are the basic and essential "building blocks" for making an almost limitless number of more interesting and intricate quilt blocks.

 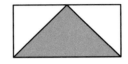

Four-patch unit   Flying Geese unit   Half-square unit

FOUR-PATCH UNITS:

- Use one light and one dark fabric strip of equal width and put them right sides together (RST).
- Sew a ¼" seam on the long side of the strips; press the seam closed first, then press the strip-set open with the seam toward the darker fabric.
- Cut the strip-set in half, rotate one unit and place it RST on top of the other unit, butting seams together and matching opposite fabrics.
- Cut into segments the same width as the cut strip width. Keep the segments RST.
- Sew the segments together along one edge. Press each unit closed first, then press open with the seam to one side.
- If you're using squares instead of strips, you will need two light and two dark squares for each four-patch unit. The squares must all be the same size.

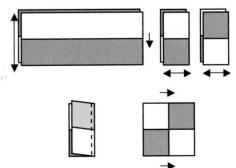

HALF-SQUARE TRIANGLES (HSTs):

This method uses the Easy Star & Geese™ Ruler

- Take one light and one dark strip of fabric of equal widths and pair them RST.
- Use Side B of the Easy Star & Geese Ruler to cut a pair of triangles according to the widths of the fabric strips. Line up the blunt edge of the ruler along the top of the strip unit and the corresponding width markings along the bottom of the strip unit. Cut.
- ROTATE the ruler 180 degrees (don't flip the ruler over; it must still be on Side B with the mint green words facing towards you) and line up the ruler along the last cut edge as shown. Cut a second pair of triangles.
- Continue in this manner until you have cut all the half-square triangle (HST) pairs needed.
- Chain stitch the units together on long edge of the triangles.
- Press the triangle units closed first, then press the units open with the seams toward the darker fabric.
- Trim the dog ears.

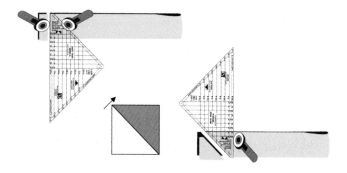

TRIPLE TRIANGLE UNITS

These are made slightly differently in PINWHEEL PUZZLE, but they're a handy little unit to know.

Place a half-square triangle and a square of the same size RST. Draw a diagonal line on the back of the square, perpendicular to the HST seam.

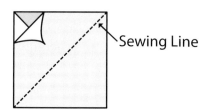
Sewing Line

Sew on the line. Lift the edge to check the color placement of the triangles. Then trim, leaving a ¼" seam allowance. Press closed, then press open.

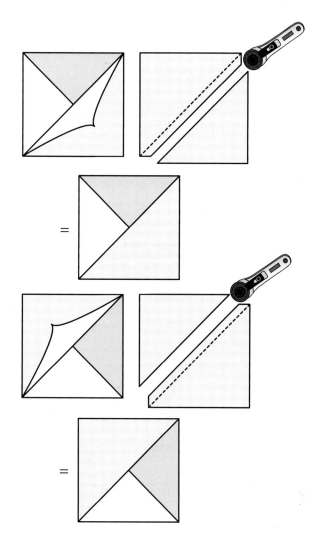

If you need identical units, see the alternate instructions on page 66.

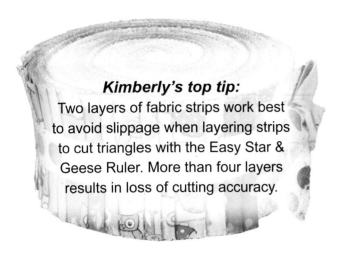

Kimberly's top tip:
Two layers of fabric strips work best to avoid slippage when layering strips to cut triangles with the Easy Star & Geese Ruler. More than four layers results in loss of cutting accuracy.

How to use the Easy Star & Geese Ruler

FLYING GEESE UNITS: No math, no wasted fabric, and no stress. Give my signature method a try. I know you'll love it!

Side A (magenta)

◎ Cut fabric strips according to the finished size of Flying Geese units listed on the left side of Side A (magenta) on the Easy Star & Geese Ruler.

◎ Line up the ruler as shown and use Side A to cut "geese" units (quarter-square triangles) from the strips.

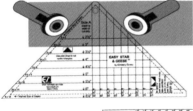

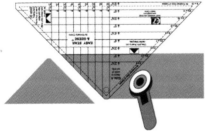

◎ Rotate the ruler 180 degrees (don't flip the ruler over; it must still be on Side A with the magenta words facing toward you) and line up the ruler along the last cut edge as shown. Cut another geese unit.

Side B (mint green)

◎ Fold the fabric strip in half right sides together (RST), and use Side B to cut "wing" units (half-square triangles) from the strips as shown. This results in mirror-image wing units.

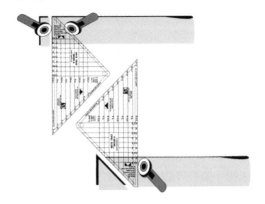

"My favorite time to make Flying Geese units is late at night, after everyone is asleep in bed, while I watch reruns of comedy sitcoms on television. I've probably made more than 10,000 Flying Geese this way and enjoyed every minute."

-- Kimberly

Flying Geese Assembly

◎ Match the notched edge of a wing unit to the notched edge of a geese unit.

◎ Place RST and sew. Always press the seam allowance toward the wing unit. Match the notched edge of an opposite side wing unit to the geese unit, place RST, and sew.

Always press the seam allowance toward the wing unit. Trim the dog ears.

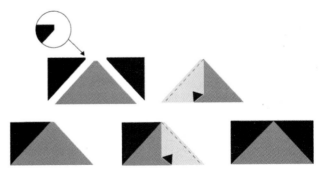

Get Set...

Number of triangles cut from one strip of fabric (based on a 42" strip):

Strip Size	# of Triangles from Side A (Geese)	# of Triangles from Side B (Wings)
2½"	14	24
3"	11	22
3½"	9	20
4"	8	18
4½"	7	16
5"	7	13
5½"	6	12
6"	5	10
6½"	5	10

The Simpli-EZ Jelly Roll Ruler

I designed a new ruler exclusively for cutting Jelly Rolls, Honey Buns, and precut fabric bundles!

When I began working on the quilts for this book, I realized that with a few exceptions, I was cutting the same basic sizes and shapes over and over—tons of 2½" squares, hundreds of 2½" x 4½" rectangles, countless 5" squares and 5" x 10" rectangles, and triangles from Layer Cakes. With my rotary cutter in one hand, I kept reaching with my other hand for two or three different standard size rulers to cut these units, depending on the type and size of units I needed to cut.

Of course you can use any good ruler to cut these simple shapes. But I began to think it might be nice to use a ruler designed specifically to make it easy to see and cut the most basic of shapes from precut strips and squares quickly and accurately. I realized I rarely (if ever!) cut any units with measurements other than whole, half, and quarter sizes to make these quilts. Eighth-inch measurements were scarcely needed!

After extensive testing and several prototypes, I unveiled the brand new, one-of-a-kind, Simpli-EZ Jelly Roll Ruler to go hand-in-hand with this book. It is designed to work with all precut fabric bundles, and it makes cutting fast and fun. It even works for left-handed quilters!

Here's why I know you'll love it too:

- It works perfectly with Jelly Rolls, Honey Buns, Charm Squares, Layer Cakes, and Turnovers.

- It allows you to cut quickly and accurately. I designed it so you can cut basic units such as squares, rectangles, and triangles from 1½" and 2½" strips, and 5" and 10" squares!

- The ruler has two-colors, which makes the markings easy-to-see and easy-to-use. The mint green "highlight" lines denote the most commonly used sizes from precut fabric strips and squares.

- There are no ⅛" lines on the ruler; only ¼", ½" and whole inch markings make viewing clear and uncluttered.

- It's just plain fun to use!

How to use the Simpli-EZ Jelly Roll Ruler:

The Simpli-EZ Jelly Roll Ruler works perfectly for both right- and left-handed quilters. The rule of thumb is easy to remember: If you are right-handed, the fabric strips will always lie to your right and you will cut left to right, as if you're reading. If you are left-handed, the fabric strips will lie to your left and you will cut from right to left. The illustrations show units being cut right-handed.

How to cut squares:

Line up the mint green highlight line along the edge of your precut strip matching the width of your strip.

Cut the square as shown.

Jelly Roll

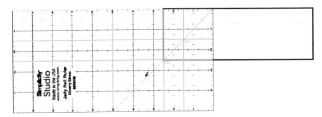

Honey Bun

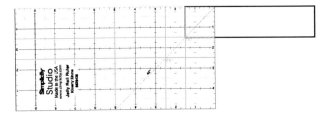

How to cut rectangles:

Line up the mint green highlight line along the edge of your precut strip matching the width of your strip.

Use the ¼", ½", or whole inch markings to cut the length of your desired unit size. Cut the rectangle as shown.

Jelly Roll

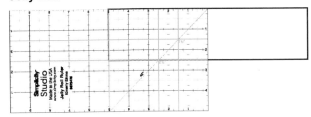

Honey Bun

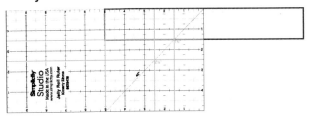

How to cut diamonds:

Line up the 45-degree line along the vertical edge of your fabric strip to cut the diamonds as shown.

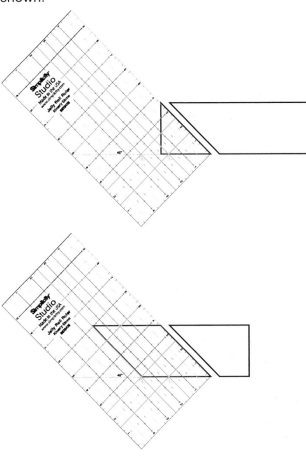

How to cut a 10" square:

Line up the ruler on one half of a 10" x 10" square. Cut in half as shown.

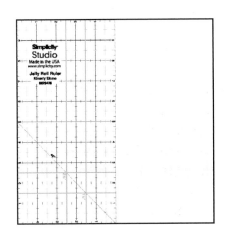

Get Set...

Use the 5" color highlight line along half of a 5" x 10" rectangle to cut perfect 5" squares as shown.

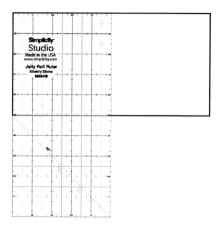

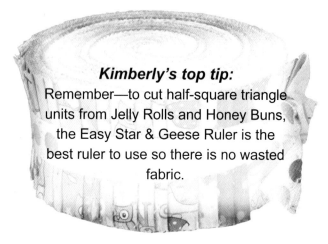

Kimberly's top tip:
Remember—to cut half-square triangle units from Jelly Rolls and Honey Buns, the Easy Star & Geese Ruler is the best ruler to use so there is no wasted fabric.

How to use the Easy Hearts™ Cut Tool:

First determine the size heart you want to cut. The chart below gives the cut size without a seam allowance. Cut a piece of fabric at least 1"–2" larger than the size heart you need. Fold the fabric in half and align the fold of the fabric along the solid line on the Easy Hearts Cut Tool.

Channel:	Size of fabric needed
Heart A	10½" x 11½"
Heart B	9½" x 9½"
Heart C	8" x 7½"
Heart D	6½" x 5½"
Heart E	4½" x 4"

Using an 18mm rotary cutter, insert the cutter in the correct groove with the blade facing the outside of the curve and begin cutting at the top of the heart at the fold line. Cut halfway around the channel and stop. While continuing to hold the Easy Hearts Cut Tool firmly with your left hand, reposition the rotary cutter so the blade is against the inner edge of the channel at the bottom of the heart. Cut from the bottom up to complete the first cut.

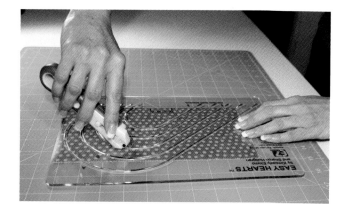

How to cut a heart in half without a seam allowance:

Determine the size heart you want, place the appropriately sized rectangles wrong sides together, and align the raw edges with the solid line on the Easy Hearts Cut Tool as shown in the diagram. Note: For the purposes of the hearts as shown in this book, the raw edges at the center of the hearts will be covered with trim or secured with decorative stitching.

How to make all the projects in this book without using the specialty rulers and tools:

I thoroughly enjoy using specialty rulers and tools when I cut fabrics in preparation for stitching. If there are specialty tools that make cutting easier, more accurate, and leave almost no wasted fabric, then color me happy! That's exactly why I designed the rulers I've demonstrated here and have shown how easy they are to use. The directions for the quilts in this book are written using these signature cutting techniques and methods, assuring you of the least amount of fabric waste when using Jelly Rolls and precut bundles. This is why I believe in my own techniques and methods so strongly.

But I realize not everyone has the ability or access to buy or use my specialty rulers, and that's quite all right. When I teach classes, I'm an instructor who never requires a student to purchase one of my rulers in order to participate in the class. I always have rulers available to lend, and I find that if a student tries my technique and method in class, nine times out of ten they'll be "Kimberly's ruler converts" by the end of class.

There's nothing wrong with using standard size rulers. At the very least, you'll need a 6½" x 24" ruler and a 12" square ruler to make the quilts in this book. However, the directions for each quilt are written with the assumption you will be using my rulers and tools to make them, and I'll tell you in the supply list at the beginning of each quilt

design which ruler(s) you should use to make that particular quilt. You can purchase my specialty rulers at most quilt shops, discount fabric stores, and at a variety of online shopping venues, or you can buy them directly from me through my Web site at www.kimberlyeinmo.com.

If you decide to use rulers you have on hand to make the quilts in this book, simply refer to this section to see how to convert the cutting instructions to use standard rulers and the more traditional methods as shown below. Please note, however, you may end up needing additional fabric to make the quilts because traditional methods for piecing half-square triangles and Flying Geese require more fabric than when using my specialty rulers and signature techniques.

How to convert the directions in this book:

To make half-square triangles (HST)

From Jelly Rolls: Cut 2½" squares from two different fabrics and layer them RST. Draw a diagonal line and stitch on the line. Trim ¼" from the stitching line and discard or set aside the trimmed triangles as they are too small for the projects in this book.

From Layer Cakes: One 10" square will make 8 triangles that will yield 4½" HST units. Trim ¼" from two adjacent sides of the 10" square then cut into 4 squares 4⅞" x 4⅞" and cut each square diagonally.

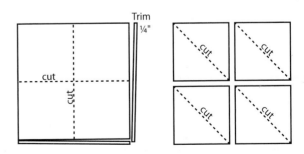

To make Flying Geese units

You can use the traditional method to make Flying Geese units. Cut two squares and one rectangle. Lay a square RST at one end of the rectangle, draw a diagonal line, and stitch on the line. After stitching, cut ¼" from the stitching line and discard or set aside the trimmed triangles as the pieces are too small for the projects in this book. Press the seam allowance toward the triangle. Repeat with the remaining square at the opposite end of the rectangle.

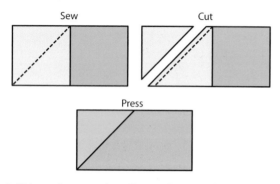

Sew   Cut

Press

Additional ways to slice a Layer Cake

Cut 4 – 5" x 5" squares to yield 4 4½" x 4½" finished squares.

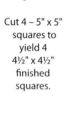

Cut 5" x 5" squares into 16 – 2½" x 2½" squares to yield 2" x 2" finished squares.

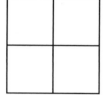

Cut twice diagonally to yield 4 8½" quarter–square finished triangles.

Cut 5" x 5" squares once diagonally to yield 8 4" finished half-square triangles.

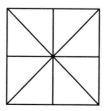

Why are there recipes in a quilting book?

Because quilting and good food go together like a needle and thread!

We've established that I'd like to be your personal quilting coach. I'll be encouraging you to try new and different things with the "Try This!" section at the end of every quilt pattern. But quilting is a lifestyle for most of us quilters. With that in mind, I just couldn't resist sharing a few of my tried-and-true, all time favorite recipes with you—just between us friends, designed to enhance your lifestyle.

Truth be told, I don't particularly enjoy cooking. In fact, my husband will tell you without hesitation that the best thing I know how to make is reservations. But honestly, I'm a good cook. So when I do actually prepare meals, I rely on my favorite recipes to save time in the kitchen so I can spend it in the sewing room. These recipes are quick and easy and are perfect to give you more time to spend doing what you love: quilting! I use them regularly, and they're not only family favorites but also big hits with my friends, which is why I know you'll love them, too. So give them a try, and I'll bet you'll soon be saying they're among your new all-time favorite recipes.

Quality Control!

Chapter Three

Sew!

Quick, easy, fast and fabulous, delectable quilts can be yours!

You've read the first two chapters, right? Is your sewing machine tuned up and ready to hum, and your sewing space all set up with notions and essential tools and rulers? Are you poised with your rotary cutter in hand and ready to jump right in and get started? Great! Because I've got some fabulous new, original quilt designs just waiting for you on the following pages.

Enough said. Let's sew!

The World's Most Versatile Quilt Block
Jacob's Ladder

If I had to choose just one quilt block as my absolute favorite, it would have to be the traditional Jacob's Ladder block. This easy, amazingly versatile block is composed of just two basic units: half-square triangles and four-patch units. But oh, the design possibilities are almost endless! The Jacob's Ladder block is a great choice for quilters of all skill levels and also the perfect place for new quilters to begin. As I said earlier, if you master the skills to make these basic piecing units, you will be able to make almost any quilt block! Simply alternating the position of the blocks results in this colorful, eye-catching quilt set in rows.

GET READY... Cutting instructions are written for use with the Easy Star & Geese Ruler.

FABRIC	YARDS	INSTRUCTIONS
1 Jelly Roll or 40 strips 2½" wide	3 yards	Select 16 medium/dark strips and cut 10 squares 2½" x 2½" from each strip (160 total) for the four-patch units. Place the remaining length of the strips RIGHT side facing up and cut 104 medium/dark Side B triangles for the Sawtooth border HSTs. Select at least 10 light strips and cut 160 squares 2½" x 2½" for the four-patch units.
1 Layer Cake or 40 squares 10" x 10"	3 yards	Separate the 10" squares into groups of lights, mediums, and darks. Set aside the light squares for another project. Cut 32 squares 4⅞" x 4⅞" from the medium and dark squares, then cut each square once diagonally to yield 64 triangles.
Background Fabric	1⅛ yards	Cut 4 squares 2½" x 2½" for the Sawtooth border cornerstones. Cut 5 strips 2½" wide. With WRONG sides facing up, cut 104 Side B triangles for the Sawtooth outer border HSTs. Cut 32 squares 4⅞" x 4⅞", then cut each square once diagonally to yield 64 triangles.
Inner Border	⅝ yard	Cut 8 strips 2½" wide and join them end-to-end.
Outer Border	1⅜ yards	Cut 8 strips 5½" wide and join them end-to-end.
Backing	4⅜ yards	Cut 2 panels 36" x 74".
Batting		74" x 74"
Binding	½ yard	Cut 7 strips 2¼" wide and join them end-to-end for the single-fold, straight grain binding.

Jacob's Ladder

Quilt size: 66" x 66"   Block size: 12" x 12"   Skill level: Easy

Jacob's Ladder

Kimberly's top tip:
When choosing light strips from your Jelly Roll, it is very important to have some contrast with your background fabric. Discard any light strips that blend too closely with your background fabric.

SEW!

Assembly Instructions

◎ Make 80 four-patch units with the light and medium/dark 2½" squares.

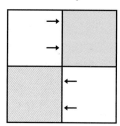

◎ Press the seams away from the light fabric.

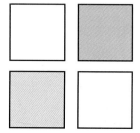

◎ The units should measure 4½" x 4½" unfinished. Square-up if necessary.

◎ Make 64 HSTs with the medium/dark and background fabric 4⅞" triangles.

◎ Press the seams away from the background fabric.

◎ The units should measure 4½" x 4½" unfinished. Square-up if necessary.

◎ Make 16 Jacob's Ladder blocks.

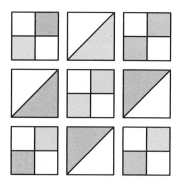

◎ Press the seam allowances as indicated by the arrows.

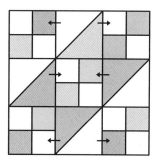

◎ Blocks should measure 12½" x 12½" unfinished. Square-up each block if necessary.

⊚ Arrange the blocks in a 4 x 4 layout as shown or in one of the Try This! layouts that follow.

⊚ Sew the blocks into rows and join the rows.

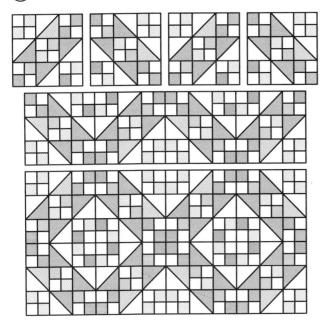

⊚ Add the inner border of 2½" strips as shown in the assembly diagram.

⊚ Make 104 HSTs with the 2½" medium/dark and background fabric triangles. The HSTs should measure 2½" x 2½" unfinished. Square-up if necessary.

⊚ Make 4 strips of 26 HSTs each. Add 2 strips to the sides of the quilt.

⊚ Add a 2½" square of background fabric to both ends of the remaining HST strips and add to the top and bottom of the quilt.

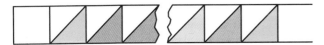

⊚ Add the outer border of 5½" strips.

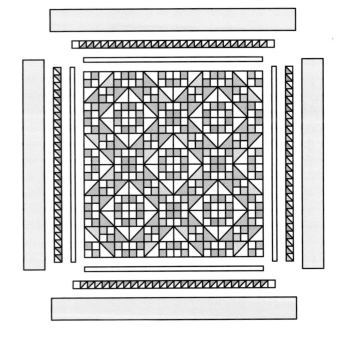

⊚ Quilt, bind, add a label, and enjoy!

TRY THIS!

Jacob's Ladder blocks are so versatile, you'll find an almost limitless number of quilt design layouts to choose from! Spend some time before you stitch your blocks together, laying them out on the floor or putting them on your design wall to pick the arrangement you love the most. To get you started, here are just a few of the possible layouts for your 16 blocks.

What's that you say? You don't have a design wall? Turn to page 51 for great ideas on how to make your own design wall for under $25!

Jacob's Ladder

JACOB'S LADDER
Layout Ideas

Take Good Advice to Heart
Half-Hearted

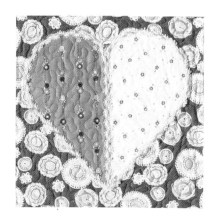

As I grew up, Mom always told me never to do anything "half-heartedly" and I took her sage advice to heart (all pun intended). I've never been a half-hearted sort of gal, preferring instead to always try to do the best I can in everything I attempt. So with the phrase "half-hearted" in my head, I designed this darling and clever quilt with a play on words in mind and one Layer Cake bundle in hand. Just for fun, you'll notice I added three extra hearts with another play on words in mind: a hole in the heart, a broken hearted, and whole-hearted. I just know you'll love this quilt with your whole heart as much as I do!

GET READY… Cutting instructions are written for use with the Easy Hearts Cut Tool.

FABRIC	YARDS	INSTRUCTIONS
1 Layer Cake or 32 squares 10" x 10"	2⅜ yards	If substituting fabric for the Layer Cake, choose an assortment of 32 different fabrics and cut a 10" x 10" square from each.
Border	¾ yard	Cut 4 strips 5½" wide and join them end-to-end.
Trims	¾ yard each of 16	Choose an assortment of braids, ribbons, rick-rack, and laces to trim the hearts. .
Backing	3¼ yards	Cut 2 panels 28" x 54".
Batting		54" x 54"
Binding	½ yard	Cut 6 strips 2¼" wide and join them end-to-end.

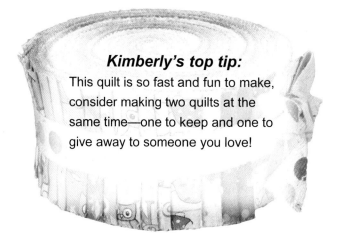

Kimberly's top tip:
This quilt is so fast and fun to make, consider making two quilts at the same time—one to keep and one to give away to someone you love!

Half-Hearted

Quilt size: 46" x 46"   Block size: 9" x 9"   Skill level: Easy

GET SET...

Additional supply list:

- Easy Hearts Cut Tool or a half-heart template (page 36)
- 18mm rotary cutter
- Assorted presser feet to accommodate couching trims
- 2½ yards Pellon® Shape Flex® lightweight fusible interfacing
- 2½ yards lightweight fusible web or basting glue (I like Appli-Glue™ by Jillily Studio.)
- 2½ yards tear-away stabilizer
- Neutral thread for stitching the blocks together
- Monofilament thread for invisible appliqué
- Selection of topstitching threads for decorative stitching (optional)

Kimberly's top tip:

Trust me when I tell you that no matter which Layer Cake line of fabric you select, the prints will look busy and mismatched as you begin to fuse the hearts onto the backgrounds. This happened to me, too. Don't be discouraged with the "clutter effect" of all the busy prints. Once you add contrasting trims or decorative stitches with bold threads to highlight your appliqué, the hearts will stand out against the busy backgrounds and you'll love the eye-popping, interesting effects you can achieve with the trims and decorative threads!

SEW!

Assembly Instructions

@ Choose 16 of the 10" x 10" squares as the background for your hearts. Arrange them in a 4 x 4 layout as shown. (Don't stitch them together yet!)

I recommend you take a digital photo of the layout so you'll be able to sew them together in this order after you have completed all the heart appliqués.

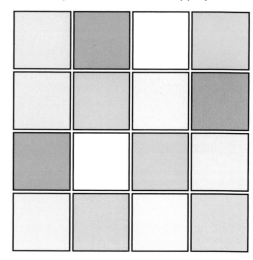

@ Cut 16 squares 10" x 10" of lightweight fusible interfacing.

@ Fuse the interfacing to the wrong side of 16 of the remaining squares following the manufacturer's instructions.

@ Cut 13 of the fusible-backed squares in half lengthwise to yield 26 rectangles 5" x 10".

@ Place 2 different rectangles WST (wrong sides together) and cut 13 pairs of mirror-image half hearts (see the templates, page 36). With the Easy Hearts Cut Tool, cut a size C half-heart using an 18mm rotary cutter.

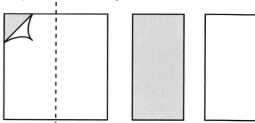

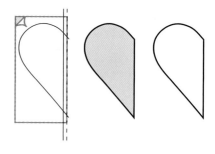

◉ Cut a heart with a hole in it, a whole heart, and two halves of a broken heart (see the templates, page 36). With the Easy Hearts Cut Tool, use sizes C and D to cut the heart with the hole.

◉ Arrange the 16 hearts on the Layer Cake squares and fuse in place.

◉ Place a 10" square of tear-away stabilizer beneath each Heart block.

◉ Stitch assorted trims, braids, ribbons, or rickrack around each heart using monofilament thread and a zigzag stitch or machine appliqué the hearts using your choice of thread and decorative stitches. Carefully remove the tear-away stabilizer.

◉ Sew the blocks into rows and join the rows.

◉ Add the border of 5½" strips.

◉ Quilt, bind, add a label, and enjoy!

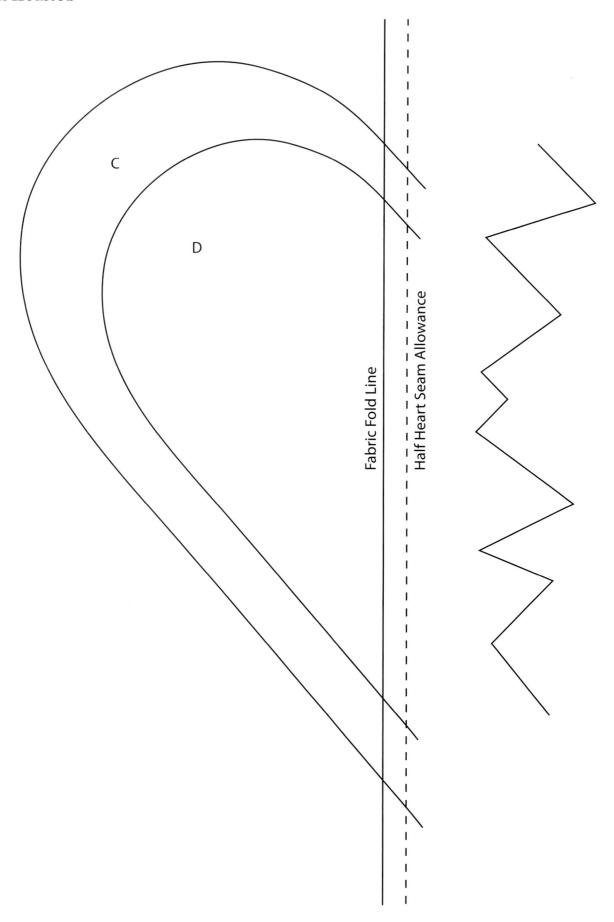

Fabric Fold Line

Half Heart Seam Allowance

C

D

TRY THIS!

Make the easiest homemade, delicious, carrot cake you'll ever taste! I'd like to share this super easy recipe, passed down to me from my mom, Nina Wallace. She can't remember where the recipe came from, but she has been making this absolutely dense and ultra-moist carrot cake for years. This cake is perfect any time of year, wins raves at potlucks and get-togethers, and is every bit as scrumptious whether you make a layer cake or serve it as a sheet cake. Give it a try and let me know how you like it!

Nina's Carrot Cake

Cake ingredients:

2 cups sugar

1½ cups vegetable oil

4 large eggs

2 cups all purpose flour

2 teaspoons baking soda

2 teaspoons cinnamon

½ teaspoon salt

3 cups finely grated fresh carrots, firmly packed

1 cup chopped walnuts

In a large bowl, cream the sugar, oil, and eggs. Mix well. Add flour, baking soda, cinnamon, and salt and mix with a spoon until all the ingredients are smooth and creamy. Add the carrots and nuts and mix well. Spray baking pans with a non-stick cooking spray. Pour batter into two 8" or 9" round pans or one large sheet cake pan. Bake at 300 degrees for one hour or until a toothpick inserted into the cake comes out clean. Cool completely before frosting.

Cream cheese frosting:

1 – 1 pound box confectioners' sugar

1 – 8 ounce package cream cheese, softened at room temperature

½ stick butter or margarine, softened at room temperature

2 teaspoons pure vanilla

Combine all the ingredients in a bowl and mix well until smooth and creamy. Do not add any additional liquid. Spread frosting over the cake and allow to set. Serve immediately or store in a cool place until serving. Enjoy!

Two Easy Blocks—One Stunning Quilt
Stars and Bars

Like a clever chameleon, this original design will look completely different depending upon the color and style of fabrics you use to make it. If your precuts are bold and bright with lots of contrast, your quilt will be dramatic and dynamic. For this quilt, I chose a soft, muted palette for a color-wash effect, like the first whispers of spring flowers after a long, cold, dreary winter. There are only a few seams to match in the Star block and no seams to match in the Bars block, so the blocks fly together quickly and easily. It's a delight to piece from beginning to end. You'll be able to whip up this pretty quilt in no time at all!

GET READY... Cutting instructions are written for use with the Easy Star & Geese Ruler.

FABRIC	YARDS	INSTRUCTIONS
2 Jelly Rolls (or 80 strips 2½" wide) OR 1 Jelly Roll (or 40 strips 2½" wide) and 1 Layer Cake (or 40 squares 10" x 10")	5⅞ yards	Choose at least 9 of the darkest strips for wings in the Flying Geese units (star points). Fold each strip RST. Cut a total of 100 pairs of Side B triangles. From the light and medium fabrics: Cut 56 Side A triangles for the geese in the Flying Geese units. Cut 152 squares 2½" x 2½" for the four-patch units and Star block corners. From the remaining fabrics: Cut 96 rectangles 2½" x 4½" for the bar units.
Background Fabric	1½ yards	Cut 3 strips 8½" wide into 48 rectangles 2½" x 8½" for the Bars blocks. Cut 3 strips 2½" wide into 48 squares 2½" x 2½" for the Star block corners. Cut 4 strips 2½" wide into 44 Side A triangles for the geese in the Flying Geese units.
Border	2¼ yards	Cut 4 strips 8½" wide along the lengthwise grain (parallel to the selvage). Allow a little extra yardage if you use a border print and plan to miter the corners.
Backing	4¾ yards	Cut 2 panels 40" x 80".
Batting		80" x 80"
Binding	¾ yard	Cut 10 strips 2¼" wide and join end-to-end for the single-fold, straight grain binding.

Stars and Bars

Quilt size: 72" x 72"   Block size: 8" x 8"   Skill level: Skilled beginner

Stars and Bars

GET SET...

Kimberly's top tip:

Trust me when I tell you it is easiest to piece your Flying Geese units for this quilt one Star block at a time and then assemble only one block at a time. To make the star point (wings) stand out, try to select different colors for your four-patch centers than what you use for the star points in each block.

Keep the star points for each block exactly the same. If you make the star points scrappy with random placement of fabrics, the blocks will not appear to be stars, but instead, a lattice of triangles and squares. Lay out the block units to ensure your colors work well before piecing them together. A design wall is very helpful for achieving a well-balanced look.

SEW!

Assembly Instructions

- Make 25 four-patch units with 100 of the light and medium 2½" x 2½" squares.

- Press the seams toward medium squares.

- The units should measure 4½" x 4½" unfinished. Square-up if necessary.

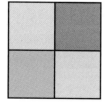

- Join 4 medium 2½" x 4½" rectangles to make the bar units as shown. Piece one block at a time so you don't end up with two matching fabric bars in the same block. Press the seams in one direction.

- Add 2½" x 8½" rectangles of background fabric to the sides to complete the Bars blocks. Make 24.

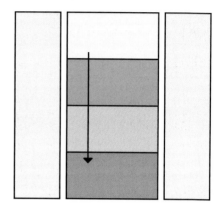

- The blocks should measure 8½" x 8½" unfinished. Square-up if necessary.

Flying Geese Assembly

- Make 100 Flying Geese units (page 19), 56 with scrappy "geese" and 44 with background fabric geese, as shown.

Make 56   Make 44

- There are three variations of the scrappy Star blocks. Pay close attention to the placement of fabrics in each block. Again, I strongly recommend that you make one block at a time so you can keep the fabric placement of each block organized.

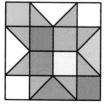 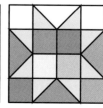 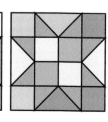

Block A   Block B   Block C
Make 20   Make 4   Make 1

◎ Make the appropriate number of each variation of Star blocks. Press the seam allowances in adjacent blocks in opposite directions so they'll nestle when you sew the blocks together.

◎ The blocks should measure 8½" x 8½" unfinished. Square-up if necessary.

◎ Sew the blocks into rows and join the rows. Press the seams open to reduce bulk.

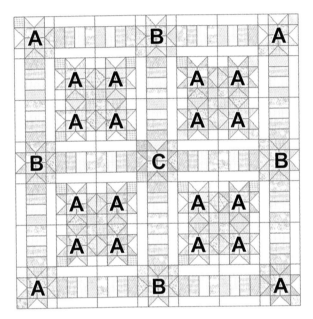

◎ Add the border.

◎ Quilt, bind, add a label, and enjoy!

TRY THIS!

Do you love the STARS AND BARS quilt but you don't want to make such a large size? Or do you need to make a beautiful quilt in a limited amount of time? STARS AND BARS is equally as lovely made in a smaller size, too! You'll only need 5 Block A scrappy Star blocks and 4 Bars blocks to make a 36" x 36" wallhanging. As a special book bonus, log onto my Web site, www.kimberlyeinmo. com, and enter the secret code AQSbook to download the complete pattern of how to make the smaller version of STARS AND BARS. *(Shhhh! The secret code is just between us friends, so mum's the word.)*

Sew Easy to Piece, So Easy to Love
Braided Links

Such a simple block, but such dramatic results! Log Cabin blocks are the perfect companions to precut fabric strips such as Jelly Rolls and Honey Buns, there's no doubt about it. This Log Cabin block variation begins in the corner instead of the center of the block so the result is a braided effect when the blocks are set side-by-side. Simply cut your 2½" strips into squares and rectangles as shown in the fabric requirements list, and let the piecing begin. You'll have a delightful lap-size quilt in no time at all that's traditional yet has a surprising twist!

GET READY... Perfect for using the Simpli-EZ Jelly Roll Ruler!

FABRIC	YARDS	INSTRUCTIONS
1 Jelly Roll or 40 strips 2½" wide	3 yards	Separate strips into two groups of light/mediums and medium/darks. Cut the pieces according to the Rotary-Cutting Chart below.
Inner Border	⅜ yard	Choose 5 strips of the same contrasting color. Cut them lengthwise into 1½" x 10½" segments. Join them end-to-end.
Outer Border	1⅛ yards	Cut 6 strips 6" wide and join end-to-end for the outer border
Backing	4⅞ yards	2 panels 32" x 81"
Batting		71" x 81"
Binding	⅝ yard	Cut 7 strips 2¼" wide and join them end-to-end for single-fold, straight grain binding.

ROTARY-CUTTING CHART

PATCH	SIZE	NUMBER OF PATCHES
A	2½" x 2½"	Cut 30 from medium/dark strips
B	2½" x 4½"	Cut 30 from medium/dark strips
C	2½" x 6½"	Cut 30 from medium/dark strips
D	2½" x 8½"	Cut 30 from medium/dark strips
E	2½" x 10½"	Cut 30 from medium/dark strips
#1	2½" x 2½"	Cut 30 from light/medium strips
#2	2½" x 4½"	Cut 30 from light/medium strips
#3	2½" x 6½"	Cut 30 from light/medium strips
#4	2½" x 8½"	Cut 30 from light/medium strips

Braided Links

Quilt size: 63" x 73"   Block size: 10" x 10"   Skill level: Easy

GET SET...

> ### Kimberly's top tip:
> When making the blocks, press the first seam allowance toward the light fabric! As you add the light/medium and medium/dark fabric strips, always press the seam allowance toward the most recently added strip. The pressing direction is very important as you set the blocks together and join the rows.

SEW!
Assembly Instructions

> ### Kimberly's top tip:
> Other than separating your strips into two piles of different color values, don't work too hard trying to make your blocks "matchy-matchy." A scrappier version is much more interesting visually. Throw caution to the wind and let the strips fall where they may!

Ⓔ Make 30 Braided Links blocks as shown, beginning with Patches A and #1. Add B, then #2, then C....and so on. Press the seams toward the last strip added.

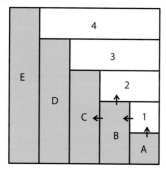

Ⓔ The blocks should measure 10½" x 10½" unfinished. Square-up if necessary.

Ⓔ Arrange the blocks in a 5 x 6 layout as shown. Sew the blocks into rows and join the rows. Press the seams open when joining the blocks to cut down on bulk.

Ⓔ Add the pieced inner border, then the outer border.

Quilt, bind, add a label, and enjoy!

TRY THIS!

Introduce the next generation of quilters to the joys of quilting.

Is there a youngster, teenager, neighbor, or friend in your life who would love to learn how to quilt? This pattern is not only easy for you to stitch up in a jiffy; it is also the perfect first project for beginning quilters!

The simple Braided Links block design allows the novice to see big results in a relatively short amount of time, and yet it is just complex-looking enough that it won't look like a beginner's first quilt. It is also a great project to practice and perfect accurate rotary-cutting skills and to hone that scant ¼" seam allowance. This block is a no-brainer when it comes to fabric selection: just ask your mentee to choose one Jelly Roll bundle she loves!

Here are a few tips to help you get organized so you can introduce your favorite pastime to a special someone in the next generation of quilters:

Make a date. Decide on a time and day to get together such as 2–3 hours every Saturday morning or one afternoon a week after school. Mark the date on your calendar and commit to meeting at regular intervals. Then stick to the plan!

Gather fun, basic sewing supplies. If you have duplicate items in your sewing studio such as multiple seam rippers, scissors, or even extra spools of neutral thread, you can put together a little basket of basic sewing supplies and surprise your mentee with a fun gift. She'll be delighted!

Surprise her! Print out a handmade coupon good for six sewing sessions or a shopping trip to your local quilt shop to help her choose fabric and supplies. Then treat her to coffee, a cold drink, or an ice cream cone to celebrate.

Start small. Set realistic goals for each of your lessons. For example, plan to get just the cutting done, and then agree to start stitching during your next meeting. You don't want to overwhelm her with too many things to learn all at once. Remember the acronym KISS (Keep it simple, sweetie!).

Offer abundant praise. She may not be able to stitch a perfect ¼" seam in the beginning, but don't be negative and discourage her first attempts. Instead, offer her praise for something she is doing right, such as sewing a straight line, trimming her threads neatly, or pressing her seams correctly. Make it fun. For the younger student, always keep it fun by making her feel like she's a "big girl" for using the grown-up sewing machine, etc. Help her with the rotary cutting (be sure to emphasize safety!) and praise her for her choice of "putting those colors together," etc.

Never discourage or offer negative feedback. There will be times when she doesn't follow your instructions exactly, or she feels discouraged because her points aren't perfect. Even during the basting process, be sure to tell her that it is just one small part of learning the process. She will improve with time and practice.

Help her with the binding. She's in the home stretch….don't let her be intimidated by the binding and allow her partially finished quilt top to languish as a UFO. Help her out, make it fun, and encourage her to finish her quilt!

Take photos. It's fun to document her progress, so be sure to take photos of her smiling and laughing along the way. Surprise her at the end of your time together with a little photo album as a memento of her graduation from novice to a veteran quilter with skills!

Treat her to lunch. Wrap up your time together and plan another shopping trip back to the quilt shop to choose more fabric for her to begin her next project.

Wrapped Up and Tied with a Bow
Cross Bows

Tied with bright, colorful ribbons and a big beautiful bow, this quilt reminds me of an exquisitely wrapped birthday present! Made with a delectable combination of Jelly Roll and Honey Bun strips plus one background fabric, this quilt will look spectacular no matter what color or style of fabrics you choose. With a little careful fabric placement planning, the colors will weave seamlessly from one block to another, creating the illusion of a complex design. Only you will know how easy it is to stitch together. You'll have this quilt wrapped up in no time!

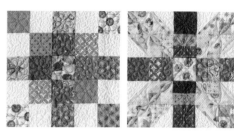

GET READY... Cutting instructions are written for use with the Easy Star & Geese Ruler.
NOTE: For this quilt, you will only need a portion of the strips from each bundle. Save the remaining strips for another project or make two quilts at once—one to keep and one to share with someone special!

FABRIC	YARDS	INSTRUCTIONS
		Separate strips into seven color groups.
		Cut 64 squares 1½" x 1½" from Color Group #3 for the four-patch units.
1 Honey Bun		Cut 32 squares 1½" x 1½" from Color Group #5 for the four-patch units.
or 11 or		Cut 32 squares 1½" x 1½" from Color Group #7 for the four-patch units.
more	½ yard	Cut 8 rectangles 1½" x 2½" from Color Group #1 for the Bow block A units.
strips 1½"		Cut 8 rectangles 1½" x 2½" from Color Group #6 for the Bow block B units.
wide		Cut 8 rectangles 1½" x 2½" from Color Group #2 for the Bow block C units.
		Cut 8 dark 1½" x 2½" rectangles from Color Group #3 for the Bow block D units.
		Cut 4 squares 2½" x 2½" from Color Group #3 for the Bow block centers.
		Cut 37 squares 2½" x 2½" from Color Group #6 for the diagonal rows in the Cross blocks.
1 Jelly Roll		Cut 8 squares 2½" x 2½" from Color Group #7 for the diagonal rows in the Cross blocks.
or 9 or more		Cut 32 Side B triangles from Color Group #5 strips for HSTs.
strips 2½"	¾ yard	Cut 12 squares 2½" x 2½" from Color Group #1 for the Bow blocks and center Cross block.
wide		Cut 40 squares 2½" x 2½" from Color Group #2 for the Bow blocks and outer Cross blocks.
		Cut 4 squares 2½" x 2½" from Color Group #5 for the center Cross block.
Background		Cut 2 strips 2½" wide into 32 Side B triangles for HSTs.
Fabric &	¾ yard	Cut 3 strips 2 ½" wide into 40 squares 2½" x 2½".
Inner Border		Cut 6 strips 2" wide and join them end-to-end for the inner border.
Outer Border	1¼ yards	Cut 4 strips 5½" wide along the lengthwise grain (parallel to the selvage).
Backing	3 yards	Cut 2 panels 25" x 51".
Batting		51" x 51"
Binding	⅜ yard	Cut 5 strips 2¼" wide and join them end-to-end for the single-fold, straight grain binding.

Quilt size: 43" x 43"   Block size: 10" x 10"   Skill level: Intermediate

Cross Bows

GET SET...

STOP! Read this first to discover the secret to making this dynamite quilt. It isn't difficult. The key to cutting and stitching the blocks with ease is to make a fabric placement legend.

Begin by sorting your colors and assigning a Color Group number to each group. Then use those numbers as you cut the units listed in the rotary cutting chart below.

Color Group	My Quilt as Shown	Your Quilt
#1	Red	
#2	Blue	
#3	Green	
#4	Background	
#5	Yellow	
#6	Orange	
#7	Light w/print	

Kimberly's top tip:

A design wall is especially helpful as you lay out the pieces for each block. Stitch one block at a time. For a truly planned quilt such as mine, pay close attention to the placement of the fabrics according to the fabric placement in the block diagrams (page 49). Choosing the darkest fabrics or fabrics with the most contrast for Color Groups #1 and #2 will help form the visual chain in the quilt and give the eye an easy path to follow.

SEW!

Assembly Instructions

Make 16 four-patch units with 32 Color Group #7 and 32 Color Group #3 1½" x 1½" squares. Press the seams open.

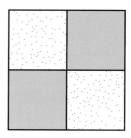

Make 16 four-patch units with 32 Color Group #5 and 32 Color Group #3 1½" x 1½" squares. Press the seams open.

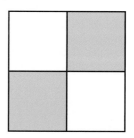

The units should measure 2½" x 2½" unfinished. Square-up if necessary.

Make 8 two-patch units with 1½" x 2½" Color Group #1 and Color Group #6 rectangles. Press the seams toward the dark rectangles.

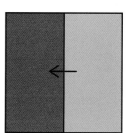

Make 8 two-patch units with 1½" x 2½" Color Group #2 and Color Group #3 rectangles. Press the seams toward the dark rectangles.

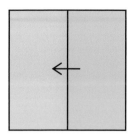

The units should measure 2½" x 2½" unfinished. Square-up if necessary.

Use 32 background fabric Side B triangles and 32 Color Group #5 Side B triangles to make HSTs for the Bow block star points. Press the seams toward the darker fabric.

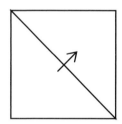

The HSTs should measure 2½" x 2½" unfinished. Square-up if necessary.

Assemble 4 Bow blocks as shown. I recommend pressing the seams open as you join the units. When units are this small, seams can be very bulky and pressing them open will eliminate some of the bulk.

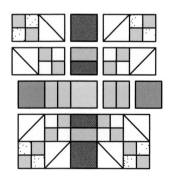

The blocks should measure 10½" x 10½" unfinished. Square-up if necessary.

Assemble 4 Cross blocks as shown, paying careful attention to the value placement of units within each block. Press the seams open.

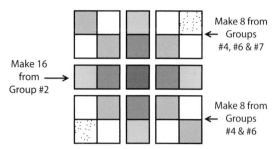

Make 8 from Groups #4, #6 & #7

Make 16 from Group #2

Make 8 from Groups #4 & #6

Choose 4 block centers from Group #6

The blocks should measure 10½" x 10½" unfinished. Square-up if necessary.

Assemble the center Cross block as shown.

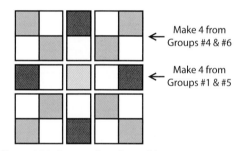

Make 4 from Groups #4 & #6

Make 4 from Groups #1 & #5

Choose 1 block center from Group #6

Arrange the blocks in a 3 x 3 layout. Sew the blocks into rows and join the rows.

Cross Bows

◉ Add the background fabric inner border.

◉ Add the outer border.

◉ Quilt, bind, add a label, and enjoy!

TRY THIS!

Design on a dime.

If you don't have a design wall or an area to arrange your pieced units and blocks, you'll soon discover how much you need one! Design walls are especially useful when making scrappy quilts or quilts constructed with many different fabrics, such as the quilts in this book. Get creative and make your own design wall for under $25. Seriously, you can do this!

Design walls can be elaborate, expensive, and prefabricated, but they certainly don't have to be. Stop at your neighborhood home building supply or hardware store or lumberyard and ask for miscuts of pressed wood, wooden planks, or even foam core board. Browse the aisles and I'll bet you'll find something that could work as the base of your design wall. Look for one that is as large as you can comfortably fit in your sewing space. My design wall is only about 30" x 60" and it sits next to my sewing cabinet when I sew.

Shop at a discount chain fabric store and buy enough white flannel to cover (with some overlap) the size of your design wall base. If you have some extra batting on hand, you may want to use a layer underneath the flannel; it makes it easier to pin blocks to the design wall. With the help of a friend, your husband, or your kids, stretch the fabric over the base and secure it tightly on the back with a staple gun. Voilà! You now have a semi-portable, inexpensive design wall. You can store it in a closet, behind a door like I do, or even under a bed when it's not in use.

I found my design wall indispensable when laying out the fabrics for this particular quilt. The quilt itself was not difficult to piece, but keeping the many different fabrics organized and arranged as I stitched the units together was a bit of a challenge. The design wall helped immensely!

Because my design wall is small and quite portable, I lean it right next to my sewing cabinet and lay out my blocks as I piece the units together, one block at a time.

As I construct each block individually, I lay out the next block to make sure the fabric placement is correct before I begin to sew.

This makes the process of assembling the quilt quick and easy, and I can see at a glance if there are any mistakes before I sew!

Star Light, Star Right
Star Chain

Simple, yet stunning. I can't think of a better description for this elegant, lovely design! Very traditional, yet with an element of originality all its own, you can piece this quilt quickly. Blended beautifully by the addition of one background fabric, this scrappy-yet-coordinated quilt requires just one Jelly Roll bundle and one Charm Pack to complete. The Star blocks are fun to stitch and they sparkle across the surface of this quilt

no matter what fabrics you choose. Simply select the two most dominant color groups from your assorted strips for the two chains that run diagonally between the Star blocks. The piano key border is the perfect complement to the blocks and uses up almost all the strips and squares, so there are few fabrics left over from your precuts to feel the least bit guilty over!

GET READY... Cutting instructions are written for use with the Easy Star & Geese Ruler.

FABRIC	YARDS	INSTRUCTIONS
1 Jelly Roll or 40 strips 2½" wide	3 yards	Separate strips into two color groups, #1 and #2. Cut 60 squares 2½" x 2½" from the Color Group #1 strips. Cut 60 squares 2½" x 2½" from the Color Group #2 strips. Cut 4 pairs of Side B triangles from 15 different strips for the wings in the Flying Geese units (120 triangles total). Cut 88 rectangles 2½" x 4½" for the piano key border.
1 Charm Pack or 19 squares 5" x 5"	½ yard	Trim 19 different 5" fabric squares to measure 4½" x 4½" for the star centers and border cornerstones.
Background Fabric	1¼ yards	Cut 7 strips 2½" wide into 60 rectangles 2½" x 4½". Cut 4 strips 2½" wide into 60 squares 2½" x 2½". Cut 5 strips 2½" wide into 60 Side A triangles for the geese in the Flying Geese units.
Backing	3⅞ yards	Cut 2 panels 29" x 64".
Batting		56" x 64"
Binding	½ yard	Cut 6 strips 2¼" wide and join end-to-end for the single-fold, straight grain binding.

Star Chain

Quilt size: 48" x 56"   Block size: 8" x 8"   Skill level: Intermediate

Star Chain

GET SET...

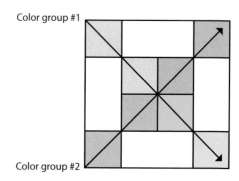

Kimberly's top tip:
Be careful and a bit frugal when cutting pieces from your strips as this pattern requires you to use almost every inch of fabric from your Jelly Roll. You will need to use rectangle units cut from the remaining Charm Pack squares to complete the piano key border.

SEW!

Chain Block Assembly

◎ Make 15 four-patch units with 30 squares 2½" x 2½" from both Color Group #1 and Color Group #2.

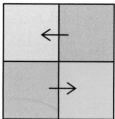

◎ Press the seams toward the darker fabric.

◎ The units should measure 4½" x 4½" unfinished. Square-up if necessary.

◎ Make 30 rectangle units with 30 squares 2½" x 2½" from both Color Group #1 and Color Group #2 and 15 rectangles 2½" x 4½" of background fabric as shown.

◎ Press the seams toward the squares.

◎ Units should measure 2½" x 8½" unfinished. Square-up if necessary.

◎ Make 15 Chain blocks as shown. Pay close attention to the orientation of color groups #1 and #2 to form the diagonals.

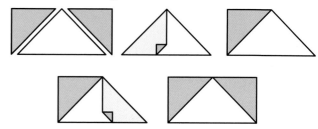

◎ The blocks should measure 8½" x 8½" unfinished. Square-up if necessary.

Star Block Assembly

◎ Make 4 identical Flying Geese units (page 19) using 4 matching pairs of Side B triangles (wings) for the star points and 4 background fabric Side A triangles (geese) (60 total). Press the seams toward the wings.

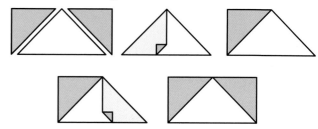

◎ The units should measure 2½" x 4½" unfinished. Square-up if necessary.

◎ Select 4½" squares of a coordinating color (but not the same fabric as star points) for the center of each block. Assemble 15 Star blocks as shown. Press seams toward the squares.

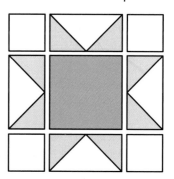

54 ————— Jelly Roll Quilts & More – Kimberly Einmo

@ Arrange the blocks in a 5 x 6 layout as shown, paying close attention to their orientation to achieve the color diagonals. Sew the blocks into rows and join the rows.

@ Join 24 rectangles 2½" x 4½" side-by-side for the side borders and 20 rectangles and 2 cornerstones 4½" x 4½" for the top and bottom borders. Add to the quilt.

@ Quilt, bind, add a label, and enjoy!

TRY THIS!

Honestly, what's not to love about slow cookers? I'm great at slow cooker meals—they are my favorites! I can throw everything into the pot first thing in the morning right after I've packed the kids' lunches for school. The ingredients simmer slowly all day long and voilà! By dinner time, I can dish out hot, tasty, delicious goodness with no muss, no fuss. Have you seen the plastic disposable liners made just for slow cookers? You can find them right between the wax paper and tin foil in your favorite grocery store. After you've enjoyed your one-pot-wonder meal, simply toss the liner into the trash. You don't even have to wash the pot! Surely these liners must have been invented by a quilter!

If you'd like a full day of guilt-free quilting AND still have a healthy, delicious, low-calorie, hearty dish of goodness for dinner, try this recipe:

Kimberly's Tasty Beef Vegetable Soup

1 pound stew beef cut in cubes

1 bag of frozen mixed vegetables (I prefer the mix of broccoli, cauliflower, and carrots, but you can certainly use whatever frozen veggies you have on hand in your freezer.)

½ bag of frozen corn

1 small onion, chopped (or 1 cup frozen chopped onion)

1 large can of tomato juice (low sodium works best)

3 beef bouillon cubes (low sodium)

Dash of salt and pepper to taste

Place all the ingredients in your slow cooker and cook on low for 8–10 hours or high for 4–5 hours. Serve with crusty French bread and slices of sharp cheddar cheese. Bon appétit!

Honey Bun Fun
Square Dance

As much as you love them, there are times when you just don't feel like cutting or stitching another triangle. And there are times when you'd rather not have to think so much about fabric placement in your blocks. If that's how you're feeling right now, this quilt is for you! This ultra-scrappy quilt is a clever partnership of one Jelly Roll, one Honey Bun, and one background fabric. Have you tried using Honey Buns yet? Sure, those 1½" strips

seem small compared to their chunkier 2½" Jelly Roll cousins, but Honey Buns open up yet another avenue of almost endless, interesting, quilt block possibilities. So pick a pair, grab your rotary cutter, and have some fun!

GET READY... Perfect for using the Simpli-EZ Jelly Roll Ruler!

FABRIC	YARDS	INSTRUCTIONS
1 Honey Bun or 40 strips 1½" wide	1¾ yards	Separate the strips into three groups of lights, mediums, and darks. Cut 200 light squares 1½" x 1½" for the four-patch units. Cut 104 medium squares 1½" x 1½" for the four-patch units. Cut 304 dark squares 1½" x 1½" for the four-patch units. Cut 52 light rectangles 1½" x 2½" for the two-patch units. Cut 52 medium rectangles 1½" x 2½" for the two-patch units.
1 Jelly Roll or 40 strips 2½" wide	3 yards	Separate the strips into three groups of lights, mediums, and darks. Cut 13 dark squares 2½" x 2½" for the Double Chain block centers. Cut 60 medium squares 2½" x 2½" for the nine-patch units. Cut 48 light squares 2½" x 2½" for the nine-patch units.
Background Fabric	1⅜ yards	Cut 7 strips 6½" wide into 100 rectangles 2½" x 6½" for the blocks.
Inner Border	⅝ yard	Cut 8 strips 2½" wide and join end-to-end.
Outer Border	1⅝ yards	Cut 8 strips 6½" wide and join end-to-end.
Backing	4⅜ yards	Cut 2 panels 38" x 74".
Batting		74" x 74"
Binding	¾ yard	Cut 9 strips 2¼" wide and join end-to-end for the single fold, straight grain binding.

Square Dance

Quilt size: 66" x 66"   Block size: 10" x 10"   Skill level: Easy

GET SET...

SEW!

Assembly Instructions

Make 100 four-patch units with 200 light (L) and 200 dark (D) squares 1½" x 1½" for the outer corners of all the blocks.

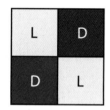

Press the seams open. The units should measure 2½" x 2½" unfinished. Square-up if necessary.

Make 12 nine-patch units with 48 light and 60 medium (M) 2½" x 2½" squares as shown.

Press the seams open. The units should measure 6½" x 6½" unfinished. Square-up if necessary.

Assemble 12 Nine-Patch Chain blocks as shown, paying careful attention to the orientation of the corner four-patch units that form the visual chain within each block.

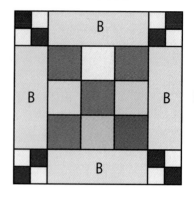

B = Background Fabric

Make 52 four-patch units with 104 medium and 104 dark squares 1½" x 1½" for the interior of the Double Chain blocks.

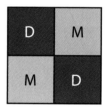

Press the seams open so the units lie flat. The units should measure 2½" x 2½" unfinished. Square-up if necessary.

Make 52 two-patch units with 52 light and 52 medium rectangles 1½" x 2½".

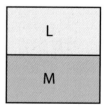

Press the seams open. The units should measure 2½" x 2½" unfinished. Square-up if necessary.

🌀 Assemble 13 Double Chain blocks as shown, again paying careful attention to the orientation of the four-patch units. Press the seams open when joining units into blocks to help them lie flat.

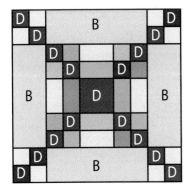

🌀 The blocks should measure 10½" x 10½" unfinished. Square-up if necessary.

🌀 Arrange the blocks in a 5 x 5 layout. Join the blocks into rows and join the rows.

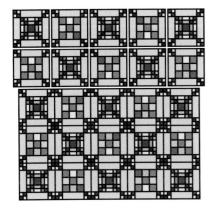

🌀 Add the inner and outer borders.

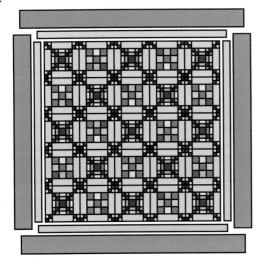

🌀 Quilt, bind, add a label, and enjoy!

TRY THIS!

It's hip to be square.

Do you take time to square-up your blocks? Sometimes referred to as "truing-up," the process is the same. Simply said, every block must be trimmed to the same size (while leaving a ¼" seam allowance) before being sewn into a quilt top. I know many quilters who skip this all-important step in a rush to assemble their quilt top only to discover their blocks are slightly askew and don't fit together nicely and precisely. Ultimately, these short-cut quilters end up ripping out their seams, defeating the purpose of skipping the squaring-up process in the first place!

Trust me when I tell you even the most advanced quilters need to true-up their blocks. No matter how accurate their seam allowance is or how carefully they piece their units, there will almost always be discrepancies that could be fixed by taking time to trim rough and uneven edges. If blocks are all trimmed to the same size before assembling the quilt top, they will stitch together cleanly with very little pinning or easing and tugging to make seam allowances and points match.

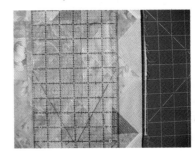

Although I was very careful to match points and sew with an accurate ¼" seam, there was still a sliver of fabric that needed trimming.

This is what was left after I squared up 16 blocks for one of my quilts. All those slivers can add up to a loss of accuracy in your completed top if they aren't trimmed first.

Internet Urban Quilt Legend
Chain Saw

I love to peruse the highways and alleys of the virtual quilt world on the Internet by way of interesting Web sites and fun-to-read quilter's blogs. Some time ago, I saw an interesting quilt pattern floating around among a number of linked blogs with a block called a Buzz Saw. The concept seemed simple enough and I filed it away in the back of my mind. When I began designing quilts for this book, the pattern again captured my imagination and I knew it would be perfect to use with a Jelly Roll and a Layer Cake. I've adapted the design and modified the block size and construction to make it compatible with precuts; however, I had hoped to track down the original

source so I could give proper credit for the concept. But alas, to no avail. My husband quipped, "That block is an Internet urban quilt legend." Perhaps, but with my own original touches, I'm calling it CHAIN SAW!

GET READY... Cutting instructions are written for use with the Easy Star & Geese Ruler.

FABRIC	YARDS	INSTRUCTIONS
1 Layer Cake or 36 squares 10" x 10"	2⅝ yards	Select 36 squares.
1 Jelly Roll from the same fabric line as the Layer Cake or 36 strips 2½" wide	2⅝ yards	Select 36 strips that match the 10" Layer Cake squares. Cut 1 rectangle 2½" x 10" from each strip (36 total). Lay the remaining strips RIGHT side facing up and cut 128 Side B triangles for the Sawtooth border. Cut 4 squares 2½" x 2½" for the border cornerstones.
Background Fabric	3⅜ yards	Cut 9 strips 10" wide into 36 squares 10" x 10". Cut 5 strips 2½" wide; lay WRONG side facing down and cut 128 Side B triangles for the Sawtooth border. Cut 3 strips 1½" wide into 6 strips 1½" x 19" for the vertical sashing. Cut 3 strips 1½" wide, join end-to-end, then cut 2 strips 1½" x 60½" for the horizontal sashing. Cut 4 squares 2½" x 2½" for the border cornerstones.
Inner Border	1 yard	Cut 8 strips 3½" wide and join end-to-end.
Outer Border	2⅝ yards	Cut 4 strips 8" wide along the lengthwise grain (parallel to the selvage).
Backing	2¾ yards 108" wide fabric	92" x 108"
Batting		92" x 92"
Binding	¾ yard	Cut 10 strips 2¼" wide and join end-to-end for the single fold, straight grain binding.

Chain Saw

Quilt size: 84" x 84"   Block size: 19" x 19"   Skill level: Skilled Intermediate

Chain Saw

GET SET...

Kimberly's top tip:
It's best to cut and piece the
Chain Saw units one at a time!

SEW!

Assembly Instructions

◉ Draw a diagonal line on the wrong side of the 10" x 10" background squares. This is the SEWING line!

◉ Pair each background square with a Layer Cake square RST.

◉ Stitch on the drawn line.

◉ Using a ruler and rotary cutter, trim ¼" beyond the sewing line.

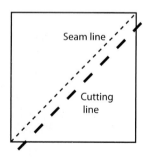

◉ Press the seam toward the Layer Cake fabric.

◉ The HST should measure 10" x 10" unfinished. Square-up if necessary.

◉ The position of each HST is very important! Make sure each block is positioned so the background fabric triangle is to the upper left as shown.

◉ Cut each HST into 4 segments 2½" wide.

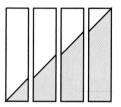

◉ Reverse the arrangement of the segments as shown.

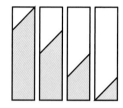

◉ Position a 2½" x 10" rectangle cut from the matching Jelly Roll rectangle to the left of the segments and sew the segments together. Press the seams toward the solid rectangle.

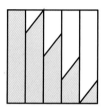

◉ The unit should measure 10" x 10" unfinished. Square-up if necessary. Make 36 units.

◉ Join 4 units together to make each Chain Saw block, as shown. Make 9.

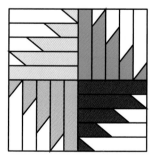

◉ The blocks should measure 9½" x 9½" unfinished. Square-up if necessary.

◉ Arrange the blocks in a 3 x 3 layout with the 1½" x 19" vertical sashing strips between the blocks. Join the blocks and sashing strips.

◎ Join the rows and the 1½" x 60½" horizontal sashing strips.

◎ Add the 3½" inner border.

◎ Make 128 HSTs using the assorted Side B triangles from the Jelly Roll and background fabrics.

Kimberly's top tip:
When making the half-square triangle border, sew your HSTs together in 16 units of 8 HSTs each. This way you can control your color and value selection and ensure you have a balanced color wave around the perimeter of your quilt. Sew 4 units together and like magic you will have completed one side of your Sawtooth border!

◎ Make 4 Sawtooth border strips of 32 HSTs each. Add 2 strips to the sides of the quilt.

◎ Add 2½" x 2½" squares to both ends of the remaining border strips and add to the top and bottom of the quilt.

◎ Add the outer border.

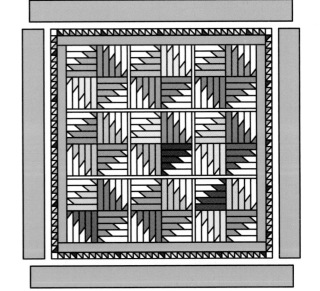

◎ Quilt, bind, add a label, and enjoy!

Fabric Magic!
Pinwheel Puzzle

Do you see any pinwheels in the block to the right? Just some Flying Geese and two sizes of triangles come together in this interesting, traditionally pieced block. But with a little planning and some clever fabric placement, the pinwheels will magically appear when the blocks are set side-by-side! It's really no puzzle at all—just follow my easy directions and clear illustrations to cut the required pieces from your Jelly Roll strips and matching Layer Cake squares and you'll piece your own beautiful Pinwheel Puzzle together in no time at all. The extra Jelly Roll strips lend themselves perfectly to make the Pinwheel patch border and with alternating scrappy squares, there are no seams to match! Fresh as a spring breeze, I know you'll love the intricate look of this quilt without having any of the fuss of complicated construction.

GET READY... Cutting instructions are written for use with the Easy Star & Geese Ruler.

FABRIC	YARDS	INSTRUCTIONS
1 Jelly Roll or 40 strips 2½" wide	3 yards	Cut 144 Side A triangles (geese)—about 4 from each strip—for the Flying Geese units. Lay the remaining strips RIGHT side facing up and cut 128 Side B triangles for the Pinwheel border blocks.
1 Layer Cake or 35 squares 10" x 10"	2⅝ yards	Choose 12 light 10" x 10" squares for the triple triangle units and trim to 7¼" x 7¼". Cut each square in half twice on the diagonal to yield 4 triangles (48 total). Choose 12 dark 10" x 10" squares for the triple triangle units and trim to 7¼" x 7¼". Cut each square in half twice on the diagonal to yield 4 triangles (48 total). Choose 11 medium 10" x 10" squares. Cut each into 4 squares 4½" x 4½" (total 44) for the block centers and borders.
Background Fabric	2⅝ yards	Cut 5 strips 6½" wide into 48 Side B triangles for the triple triangle units. Cut 12 strips 2½" wide; fold each strip RST and cut 144 PAIRS of Side B triangles (wings) for the Flying Geese units. Cut 11 strips 2½" wide. Lay WRONG side facing up and cut 128 Side B triangles (wings) for the Pinwheel border blocks.
Inner Border	½ yard	Cut 6 strips 2½" wide. Join end-to-end.
Backing	5 yards	Cut 2 panels 34" x 84".
Batting		68" x 84"
Binding	⅝ yard	Cut 7 strips 2¼" wide; join end-to-end for the single-fold, straight grain binding.

Pinwheel Puzzle

Quilt size: 60" x 76"   Block size: 16" x 16"   Skill level: Intermediate

Pinwheel Puzzle

GET SET...

SEW!

Assembly Instructions

@ Construct triple triangle units using 1 light Layer Cake triangle, 1 dark Layer Cake triangle, and 1 large background fabric triangle. Pay close attention to the position of each patch within the square as shown in the diagram. Make 4 of each color combination (48 total).

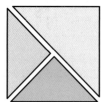

@ The units should measure 6½" x 6½" unfinished. Square-up if necessary.

Flying Geese Assembly

@ Make 144 Flying Geese units (page 19) with the 144 small Jelly Roll Side A triangles (geese) and the 144 PAIRS of background fabric Side B triangles (wings).

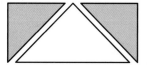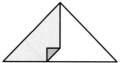
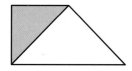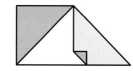

@ Each unit should measure 2½" x 4½" unfinished. Square-up if necessary.

@ Make 12 Pinwheel Puzzle blocks with the Flying Geese, triple triangle units, and center squares as shown. Pay careful attention to your fabric placement of the corner triple triangle units in your blocks so they will match at the intersection of each block to form the large pinwheels. Use a design wall or board to help you lay out your block units to achieve this effect.

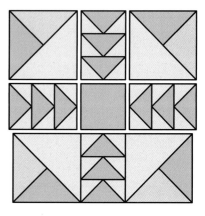

@ The blocks should measure 16½" x 16½" unfinished. Square-up if necessary.

@ Make 32 small Pinwheel blocks for the border with the Jelly Roll and background fabric Side B triangles as shown.

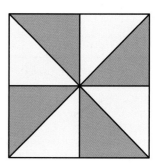

@ The blocks should measure 4½" x 4½" unfinished. Square-up if necessary.

@ Arrange the Pinwheel Puzzle blocks in a 3 x 4 layout being careful to match the pinwheels at the block intersections. Sew the blocks into rows and join the rows. The quilt top should measure 48" x 64".

@ Add the 2½" wide inner border. The quilt top should now measure 52"x 68".

@ Join 8 Pinwheel blocks and 9 Layer Cake squares 4½" x 4½" for the side borders and 8 Pinwheel blocks and 7 Layer Cake squares for the top and bottom borders. Add to the quilt.

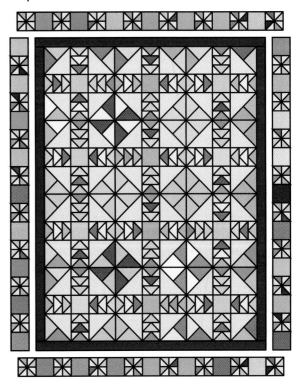

@ Quilt, bind, add a label, and enjoy!

TRY THIS!

The Top 10 things to do to "jumpstart" creativity and get your mojo back!

As a quilt designer, I experience periodic creative ups and downs. On most days, I may have dozens of new designs in my mind and can't get them down on paper fast enough. There are other times, though, when I just can't seem to create any new, exciting ideas or original designs. Similar to a writer suffering from writer's block, I think all quilters go through phases of feeling uninspired to either begin a new quilt or finish a top in progress. Or perhaps you just feel so overwhelmed with the tasks at hand you just don't know where to start.

Just for fun, I thought I would share with you my list of top 10 favorite things to do to get the creative juices flowing again, à la late night television host style!

#10 Tidy up your sewing space and make a fresh start. It's hard to feel creative and inspired when you have remnants of fabric and supplies from previous projects lying about the room. Take time to get organized, empty your trash can, toss unusable scraps, and clear your sewing area of clutter so you can think clearly. Nothing inspires quite as much as a fresh, clean palette!

#9 Change the beat. I frequently listen to music while I'm working in my studio and I enjoy a wide variety including classical, contemporary Christian, easy listening, Southern gospel, even vintage Patsy Cline. But if I'm in a rut, one of the best things I can do to shake up the routine a bit is to change the tunes on my CD player or my iPod. New music wakes up my senses and makes me "think outside the box."

#8 Search the Internet. Spend a few hours surfing the Web for new trends in quilting, fabric lines, and even new techniques. Read your favorite quilter's blogs and click on new links to take a peek at what other quilters are working on. Seeing other people's creativity can be a big boost! If you're in a color rut, check out this Web site, http://www.adobe.com/products/kuler/, where you can experiment and try an unlimited number of color combinations sure to spark your creativity and help you choose a bold new color combo for your next project.

#7 Peruse old books and magazines. I'll just bet you have a stack of quilt magazines lying around, stored in a basement or attic, or perhaps a shelf full of books you haven't looked at in years. Make yourself a cup of tea, get comfy in your favorite chair, and spend the afternoon flipping through the pages again. I'll bet you'll come across several quilts you always "planned" to make but never got around to. Now's the time! If your tastes have changed and your own books no longer appeal to you, why not donate them to your guild's library or organize a book swap with your friends?

#6 Invite a friend for a day of stitching. Nothing helps inspire creativity or gets your momentum going again quite like spending the day sewing with a friend. You'll end up chatting, laughing, and bouncing ideas off each other and the day will pass much too quickly. But more importantly, you will have accomplished some sewing and perhaps you'll even finish a project.

#5 Visit your local quilt shop and splurge on one new thing. Give yourself a "creativity jumpstart budget" of $5–$10 and go shopping! Search for one new thing within your budget such as a spool of decorative thread, a new notion or tool, a pack of Charm Squares, or even some new sewing machine needles. Just the act of going to the shop and browsing will trigger your mind to think in a different, new, and exciting direction.

#4 Finish a project. If you have some UFOs lying around, determine to finish at least one of them. It could be a task such as stitching the binding down or something as small as adding a label to the back of a quilt. Free up your mind and lighten the burden by checking a UFO off your list of things to do!

#3 Experiment with quilt design software. There are many wonderful software packages on the market today geared just for quilters. If you haven't used them before, teach yourself by letting the tutorials guide you or ask a friend to show you how to use the software. Search for blocks you've never made or try a unique setting. Whether or not you actually construct the quilt isn't important. The process of arranging the blocks and settings on the computer screen will set your mind in motion.

#2 Sort through your stash. You probably have fabric in your stash you forgot you own! (Yes, I'm speaking from experience.) Take time to reacquaint yourself with the fabrics you have on hand; get them organized. Mix and match different color combinations. Pull out any "ugly" fabrics you can't remember why you bought, and donate them to your guild or organize an ugly fabric swap with your friends. Just play and have fun with your fabrics!

#1 Begin a new quilt from this book using Jelly Rolls and precuts! (OK, I just had to throw this one in because making these quilts is so much FUN!)

Scrappy Exuberance
Diamond Chain

This scrappy quilt dances with charm and exuberance! Depending on the delicious combination of Jelly Roll and Honey Bun strips you select, your version of this pattern will have a gorgeous, custom-designed look all its own. The outer pieced border only looks complex; it is actually just one simple double Four-Patch block rotated to achieve the pretty chain. This stunning design will draw lots of "oohs" and "ahs" from your friends during show and tell at your next guild meeting. So what are you waiting for? Start cutting your strips today!

GET READY... Cutting instructions are written for use with the Easy Star & Geese Ruler.

FABRIC	YARDS	INSTRUCTIONS
1 Jelly Roll or 40 strips 2½" wide	3 yards	Choose 13 medium or dark strips and fold RST. Cut 4 PAIRS of Side B triangles (wings) from each strip for the Flying Geese units (star points) (104 triangles total). Choose 12 medium or dark strips (can be same or different strips as used for stars). Cut 4 Side A triangles (geese) from each strip for the Flying Geese units (diamond points) (48 triangles total). Cut 100 squares 2½" x 2½" for the large four-patch units. Lay the remaining strips right-sides up and cut 64 Side B triangles for the HSTs.
1 Honey Bun or 40 strips 1½" wide	1¾ yards	Cut a rectangle 1½" x 11" from each of 40 strips (40 total).
Background Fabric	1¾ yards	Cut 5 strips 2½" wide into 72 squares 2½" x 2½". Cut 3 strips 2½" wide, lay with right side facing DOWN, and cut 64 Side B triangles for HSTs. Cut 2 strips 11" wide into 40 rectangles 1½" x 11". Cut 4 strips 2½" wide into 52 Side A triangles (geese) for the Flying Geese units. Cut 2 strips 2½" wide, fold RST, and cut 48 Side B triangles (wings) for the Flying Geese units.
Backing	3⅜ yards	Cut 2 panels 28" x 56".
Batting		56" x 56"
Binding	⅓ yard	Cut 5 strips 2¼" wide and join end-to-end for the single-fold, straight grain binding.

Diamond Chain

Quilt size: 48" x 48"   Block size: 8" x 8"   Skill level: Intermediate

Diamond Chain

GET SET... SEW!

Assembly Instructions

◉ Make 25 four-patch units with 100 assorted squares 2½" x 2½". Press the seams toward the darker fabric.

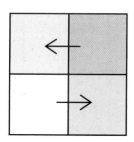

◉ The units should measure 4½" x 4½" unfinished. Square-up if necessary.

◉ Make 40 strip-sets by joining 40 Honey Bun and 40 background fabric 1½" x 11" rectangles RST together. Press the seams toward the Honey Bun strips.

◉ Cut 7 segments 1½" wide from each strip-set (total 280).

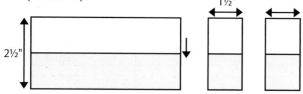

◉ Mix up the segments and make 140 small four-patch units.

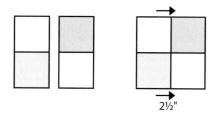

◉ The units should measure 2½" x 2½" unfinished. Square-up if necessary.

◉ Make 64 HST units with 64 Jelly Roll and 64 background Side B triangles. Press the seams toward the Jelly Roll fabric.

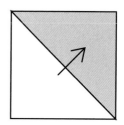

◉ The units should measure 2½" x 2½" unfinished. Square-up if necessary.

◉ Set aside 16 HSTs for the pieced border blocks and 48 HSTs for the Diamond blocks.

Flying Geese Assembly

◉ Make 13 matching sets of 4 Flying Geese units (page 19) using 4 matching pairs of Side B triangles (wings) and 4 Side A triangles (geese) of background fabric (52 total). Press the seams toward the wings.

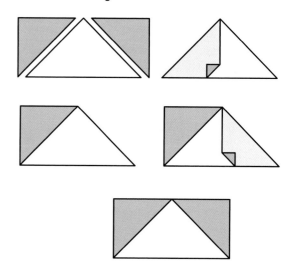

◉ The units should measure 2½" x 4½" unfinished. Square-up if necessary.

Ⓐ Assemble 13 Star blocks as shown. Press the seams open.

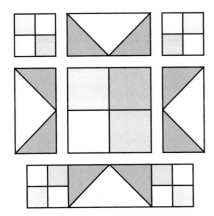

Ⓐ Assemble 12 Diamond blocks as shown. Press the seams open as you join the units.

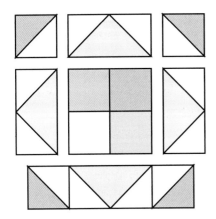

Ⓐ Arrange the blocks in a 5 x 5 arrangement as shown. Sew the blocks into rows and join the rows.

Ⓐ Make 28 double Four-Patch blocks and 16 Four-Patch/HST blocks for the border as shown. Pay close attention to the orientation of the HSTs within the block. Press the seams open as you join the units.

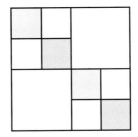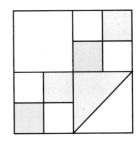

Ⓐ Blocks should measure 4½" x 4½" unfinished. Square-up if necessary.

Diamond Chain

@ Add pieced border blocks, paying careful attention to the placement and rotation of the blocks to achieve the overall secondary design.

@ Quilt, bind, add a label, and enjoy!

TRY THIS!

Best Brownies Ever!

OK, here's a super quick recipe I know you're going to love. Do you ever need a crowd-pleasing dessert in a hurry but simply don't have time to make something from scratch? These home-baked brownies are the best ever—you'll get rave reviews and they take only minutes to mix and make.

Buy the "Supreme Brownie" brand mix that includes the packet of chocolate syrup in the box. (This is important!) Mix as directed BUT (here are the super secret differences!) add 3 large eggs instead of 2 and ½ cup instead of ⅓ cup of vegetable oil. Bake as directed and allow to cool in the pan for less than 5 minutes. Frost the entire pan of brownies using chocolate fudge frosting from a can while the brownies are still warm. The frosting will melt into the brownies and make them extra dense and moist! Allow the frosted brownies to cool thoroughly. Cut and serve. I guarantee these will disappear in a flash. Yummy!

Chapter Four

Fast and Fun—
Done with One!

Also known as One Block Wonders, here are four quick and easy little quilts to whip up in a jiffy using just one wonderful block or unit!

Fast and simple, fun and fabulous, give these quilts a try when you just want to play with your precuts, stitch happily along, and not think or plan too much! Follow my no-fuss directions and get right to the good stuff.

Log Cabin Block
Honey Bun Cabins

Fast facts at a glance:

One unit: rectangles and squares from Honey Bun strips
Block size: 7" x 7"/36 blocks
Quilt size: 54" x 54"
Skill level: Beginner/Easy

GET READY... Perfect for using the Simpli-EZ Jelly Roll Ruler

FABRIC	YARDS	INSTRUCTIONS
2 Honey Buns or 80 strips 1½" wide	3½ yards	Separate strips into two color groups of lights and darks. Divide your medium strips between the two groups. Cut the pieces according to the Rotary Cutting Chart below.
Border	1⅝ yards	Cut 4 strips 6½" wide lengthwise (parallel to the selvage).
Backing	3¾ yards	Cut 2 panels 32" x 62".
Batting		62" x 62"
Binding	½ yard	Cut 6 strips 2¼" wide and join end-to-end for the single-fold, straight grain binding.

ROTARY-CUTTING CHART

PATCH	LOGS	FOR EACH 7" BLOCK, CUT
A	1½" x 1½"	1 light, 1dark
B	1½" x 2½"	1 light, 1 dark
C	1½" x 3½"	1 light, 1 dark
D	1½" x 4½"	1 light, 1 dark
E	1½" x 5½"	1 light, 1 dark
F	1½" x 6½"	1 light, 1 dark
G	1½" x 7½"	1 light

Honcy Bun Cabins

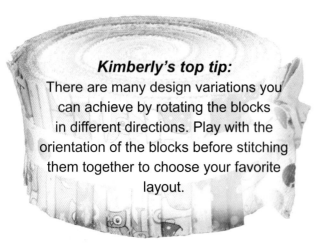

Kimberly's top tip:
There are many design variations you can achieve by rotating the blocks in different directions. Play with the orientation of the blocks before stitching them together to choose your favorite layout.

SEW!

Assembly Instructions

- Assemble the Log Cabin blocks as shown, beginning with the two A patches and adding the pieces in sequence. Always press the seams away from the center, toward the last log added.

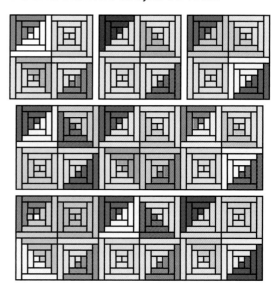

- The blocks should measure 7½" x 7½" unfinished. Square-up if necessary.

- Make 9 units of 4 Log Cabin blocks each as shown.

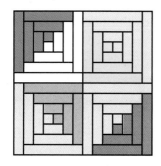

- The units should measure 14½" x 14½" unfinished. Square-up if necessary.

- Arrange the units in a 3 x 3 layout as shown. Sew the units into rows and join the rows.

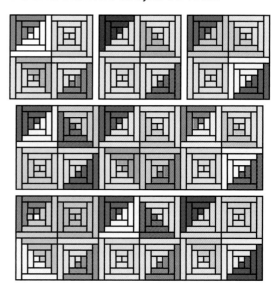

- Add the border.

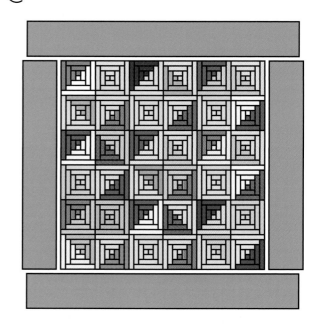

- Quilt, bind, add a label, and enjoy!

TRY THIS!

My secret family recipe for Nuts and Bolts:

My mom and I have been making Nuts and Bolts every Christmas since I was a little girl. I'm not sure where she found the original recipe, but over the years, we've added a little bit here or deleted an ingredient there until we came up with the version of the recipe we use today. It's a savory, little-bit-spicy version of the traditional party mix. But our version is oh-so-much tastier!

These days we don't wait for Christmas to make this lip-smackin' snack treat. It's perfect any time of the year and is especially great to share with friends during a weekend quilt retreat when you're stitching into the wee hours of the morning! Every time we make it, the house is filled once again with that familiar aroma of garlic, Tabasco, and Worcestershire. Yummo!

This recipe is just too delicious not to share. So, put on your apron and whip up a few batches of this munchy goodness for your family or for your next guild meeting. It won't last long around your house or at refreshment time. I just know you'll love it!

Kimberly's top tip:
I like to make multiple batches at the same time. I measure the dry ingredients listed into gallon size zip closure bags. Then I'll pour one bag at a time into a large mixing bowl, add the mixture of wet ingredients, toss to coat, and bake. When thoroughly cooled, back each batch goes into its own bag.

Kimberly's Nuts and Bolts

Preheat oven to 350 degrees.

Mix in bowl:
1½ cups of Rice Chex® cereal
1½ cups of Corn Chex® cereal
1 cup of Wheat Chex® cereal
2 cups of pretzel sticks
1½ cups of Cheerios® cereal
⅔ cup Spanish peanuts
⅔ cup cashew halves and pieces

Combine:
¼ cup melted margarine
¼ cup vegetable oil
2 teaspoons garlic powder
1 teaspoon Lawry's® Seasoned Salt
3 tablespoons Worcestershire sauce
1 teaspoon Tabasco® Sauce (or more, to taste)

Pour the liquid mixture over the crunchy mixture. Toss thoroughly to coat. Spread out on a large baking sheet lined with aluminum foil. Bake at 350 degrees for 6 minutes. Remove from the oven, stir thoroughly. Bake another 6 minutes. Pour out on flat brown paper grocery bags to soak up excess oil. Let cool thoroughly. Store in gallon size storage bags. Enjoy!

Arc Block
Charming Circles

Fast facts at a glance:

One unit: appliquéd arcs from Charm Pack squares
Block size: 4½" x 4½"/16 blocks
Quilt size: 22" x 22"
Skill level: Beginner/Easy

GET READY...

FABRIC	YARDS	INSTRUCTIONS
2 Charm Packs or 32 squares 5" x 5"	⅝ yard	Choose 16 squares for your background. Choose 16 squares for the arc appliqués.
Inner Border	¼ yard	Cut 3 strips 1½" wide and join end-to-end.
Outer Border	—	Cut 42 squares 2½" wide for the outer border. Save the remaining Charm Pack squares or scraps for another project.
Fusible Web	½ yard	
Tear-away Stabilizer	½ yard	
Backing	⅞ yard	30" x 30"
Batting		30" x 30"
Binding	¼ yard	Cut 3 strips 2¼" wide and join end-to-end for the single-fold, straight grain binding.

Charming Circles

GET SET... SEW!

⊚ Assembly Instructions

Trace 16 arcs (page 83) onto the paper side of the fusible web. Cut out beyond the drawn line and fuse to the wrong side of 16 Charm squares.

⊚ Cut out the arcs on the drawn line.

⊚ Fuse the arcs in place on 16 background patches as shown.

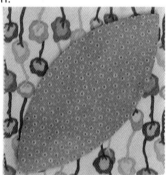

⊚ Place a 5" x 5" square of tear-away stabilizer beneath each block.

⊚ Outline the arcs with a dense satin or decorative stitch with a high contrast thread. Carefully remove the stabilizer after stitching.

⊚ Arrange the blocks in a pleasing 4 x 4 layout, paying careful attention to orientation of the arcs. Sew the blocks in rows and join the rows.

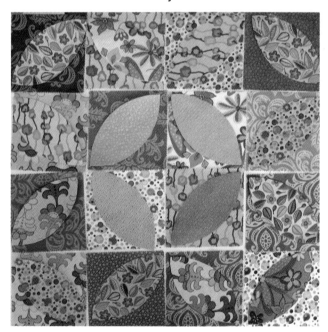

Kimberly's top tip:

Most Charm Packs are filled with a variety of very busy fabrics and only a few "blenders." Don't be discouraged by the lack of color value or contrast between the prints. As you're combining arcs with background squares, they may even appear to clash. Use them anyway! Notice in the photo my units in progress and the lack of definition between the squares and arcs. Don't worry! Simple decorative or satin stitching using a thread color with high contrast will make the arcs stand out and your circles will almost magically appear!

◎ Add the inner border.

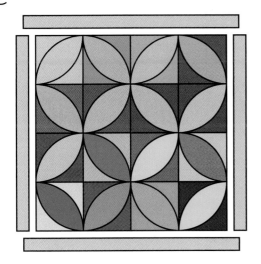

◎ Sew together 10 squares 2½" x 2½" for the side outer borders and add to the quilt. Sew together 12 squares 2½" x 2½" for the top and bottom outer borders and add to the quilt.

◎ Quilt, bind, add a label, and enjoy!

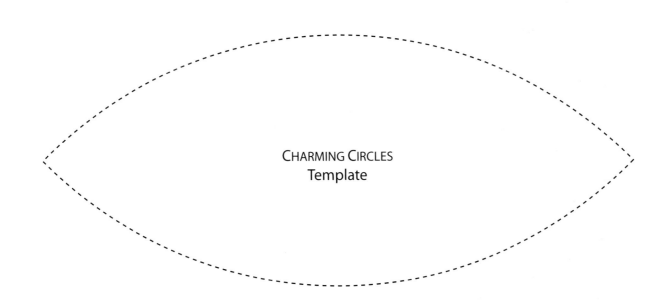

CHARMING CIRCLES
Template

Zigzag Triangles
Lightning Strike

Fast facts at a glance:

One unit: triangles cut from Jelly Roll strips
Strip unit size: 13 triangles from each strip
# of strips: 17
Quilt size: 39" x 42"
Skill level: Skilled beginner

GET READY... Cutting instructions are written for use with the Easy Star & Geese Ruler.

FABRIC	YARDS	INSTRUCTIONS
1 Jelly Roll or 40 strips 2½" wide	3 yards	Choose 15 strips for the triangle zigzags. Cut 1 pair Side B triangles from 14 strips (14 pairs total). Cut 13 Side A triangles from the remainder of each of the 15 strips (195 total). Cut 2–3 rectangles 2½" x 4½" from each of the remaining 25 strips for the outer border (62 total).
Inner Border	¼ yard	Cut 4 strips 1½" wide and join end-to-end. Cut 4 squares 4½" x 4½" from scrap fabric for the border cornerstones.
Backing	2⅜ yards	Cut 2 panels 24" x 48".
Batting		48" x 48"
Binding	⅓ yard	Cut 5 strips 2¼" wide and join end-to-end for the single-fold, straight grain binding.

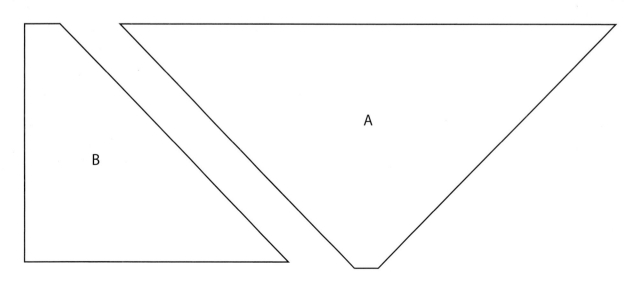

Lightning Strike

Lightning Strike

GET SET...

Kimberly's top tip:
This quilt is perfect for using up leftover strips from other projects. You can enlarge the quilt simply by adding more triangles in each row or by adding more rows.

SEW!

Assembly Instructions

◉ Lay out matching triangles in adjacent rows to create the zigzag design. Sew the triangles together, one row at a time. Press the seams in each row in the same direction, then press the seams in the neighboring row in the opposite direction.

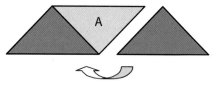

◉ Add Side B triangles to the ends of each row.

◉ Join the rows, making sure to maintain the zigzag design.

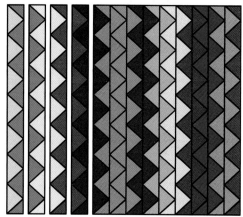

◉ Add the inner border. Press the seams toward the border strips.

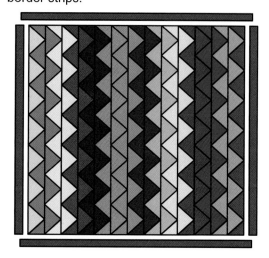

◉ Make 2 strips of 15 rectangles each, 2½" x 4½", sewn side-by-side for the piano key border.

◉ Add to the sides of the quilt.

◉ Make 2 strips of 16 rectangles each, 2½" x 4½", and add 4½" x 4½" squares to both ends. Add to the top and bottom of the quilt.

◉ Quilt, bind, add a label, and enjoy!

TRY THIS!

Cheeseburger Soup

Everyone loves this tasty soup – especially kids!

Prep time: 20 minutes

Cook: 8–10 hours on low or 4–5 hours on high in your slow cooker; can also be made on stove top.

Makes six servings

1 – 1½ pounds ground beef
1 yellow onion chopped
2 tablespoons minced garlic
1 small bag frozen cut carrots
1 large potato cubed (optional)
2 – 10.75 cans condensed cheddar cheese soup

2 – 14 ounce cans beef broth
¼ cup ketchup
¼ cup yellow mustard
1 teaspoon salt
½ teaspoon black pepper
½ cup shredded cheddar cheese
1 dill pickle diced (optional)

Brown the ground beef, onion, and garlic in a skillet and drain off the excess fat. Place the beef mixture and all remaining ingredients except shredded cheddar cheese and pickle in your slow cooker. Stir to combine. Cover and cook on low or high heat as noted above. Top each serving with shredded cheese and pickle. Serve and enjoy!

Leftovers
Bricks

Fast facts at a glance:

One unit: rectangles and squares from Jelly Roll strips
Block size: 16" x 16"/20 blocks
Quilt size: 64" x 80"
Skill level: Beginner/Easy

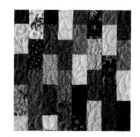

GET READY... Perfect for using the Simpli-EZ Jelly Roll Ruler!

FABRIC	YARDS	INSTRUCTIONS
2 Jelly Rolls or 80 strips 2½" wide	6 yards	For each block, cut 28 rectangles 2½" x 4½" (560 total) and 8 squares 2½" x 2½" (160 total).
Backing	5¼ yards	Cut 2 panels 36" x 88".
Batting		72" x 88"
Binding	⅝ yard	Cut 8 strips 2½" wide and join end-to-end for the single-fold, straight grain binding.

GET SET... SEW!
Assembly Instructions

◎ For each block, make 4 strips of 4 rectangles 2½" x 4½" sewn together end-to-end as shown. Press the seams in the same direction.

◎ Make 4 strips of 3 rectangles and 2 squares 2½" x 2½" sewn together end-to-end as shown. Press the seams in the same direction.

◎ DO NOT match seams! (How many times in a quilt book will you ever read "do not match seams?")

◎ Sew the 8 strips together, alternating them as shown. Make 20 blocks.

◎ Arrange the blocks in a 4 x 5 layout with all the blocks oriented in the same direction or rotating the alternate blocks 90 degrees. Choose whichever design you like best!

◎ Quilt, bind, add a label, and enjoy!

Bricks

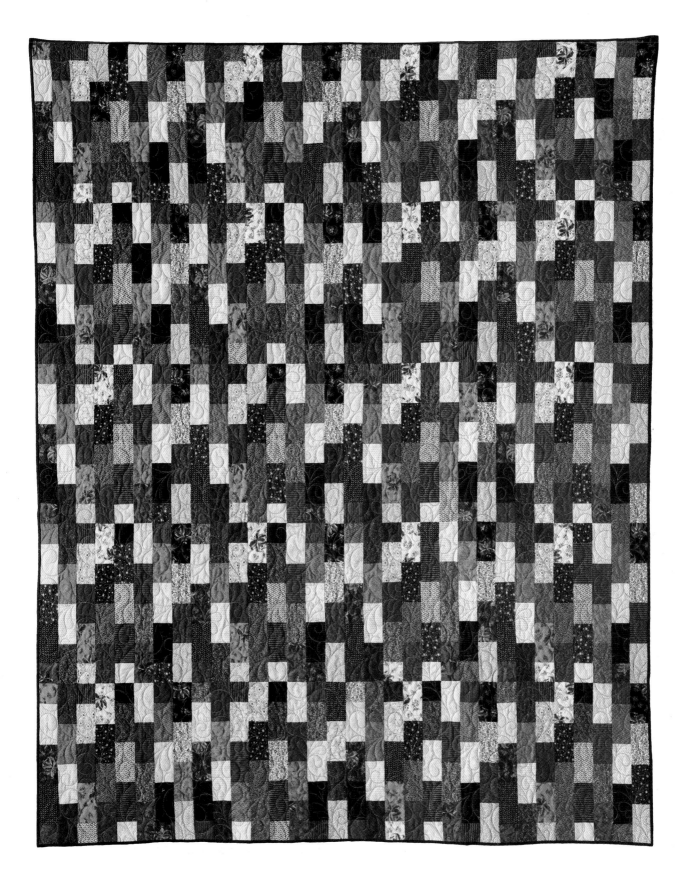

Chapter Five

Fun with Friends!

From left to right: Birgit Schüller, Carla Conner, yours truly, and Ilona Baumhofer

How to host a fun-filled Jelly Roll Retreat

In designing the quilts and writing the patterns for this book, I realized I needed to bounce my design ideas off a few of my quilting buddies to make sure the patterns were quilter-tested and road-ready. So I planned the first-ever Jelly Roll Retreat here in my home and invited them to come for a stress-free weekend of sewing fun to play with precut bundles and stitch the patterns. While we actually sewed like crazy all weekend long, we also shared heaps of fun and laughter and we all felt re-energized and inspired with creativity by the end of the weekend. So I thought I'd share several ideas for organizing your own Jelly Roll Retreat so you, too, can experience the excitement of quilting with precuts while having fun with your friends!

Rotary cutters ready to go...

Be a trendsetter. Be the first among your friends to host a Jelly Roll Retreat! Quilters are always on the lookout for the next "big thing" and this is IT! In these tough economic times we need creative outlets and inexpensive ways to socialize. That's one of the many reasons why Jelly Rolls, Honey Buns, Layer Cakes, and other precut fabrics are such a big hit; they give quilters the most bang for their buck! Hosting a Jelly Roll Retreat will allow you to combine all your favorite things in a fun-filled, jam-packed weekend without breaking the bank!

Plan now, play later

A little advance planning will allow you to actually be able to sew and enjoy the retreat. Begin by choosing a weekend about six weeks to two months in advance to allow your invitees plenty of time to make arrangements to attend.

Think about your guest list. How many people do you plan to invite? Will they spend the night or sleep in their own homes and return the next day? How many can fit comfortably in the space you have available for sewing? You may need to commandeer the family rec room or living room for the weekend. Moving the furniture around to allow ample seating and room to spread out is important. Don't invite more friends than can fit comfortably. If seating or work space is limited, frustrations may run high and no one will have a good time. Keep your expectations realistic.

I invited three good friends to my Jelly Roll Retreat, not only because that's how many beds I had available, it was also the perfect number to fit comfortably in my studio. We had plenty of room for everyone to set up their sewing machines and one iron for every two people. It was not only the perfect fit in a practical sense; it was a perfect fit of compatible personalities. You'll want to consider the different personality types of those you plan to invite as well. In other words, invite friends with similar interests and temperaments. The last thing you need is tension in the air because two or more guests end up squabbling.

Will you need extra tables and comfy chairs? Consider borrowing these from your local school or church, or ask people to bring their own. You may even ask them to bring their own pillow for extra back support during those late night sewing sessions. The key is to plan ahead. (Of course, there's nothing wrong with being spontaneous. If you feel like it, call your gal pals on a Thursday and invite them for the weekend. You can work out the details as you go!)

Jelly Rolls, Honey Buns, and Layer Cakes, oh my!

This retreat is all about making quilts with the fabulous patterns in this book using precuts, spending time with your friends, noshing on great food, and laughing all weekend long. With that in mind, prior to the retreat, ask everyone to get their own copy of this book and have them each select a project. Did you know I'll sign and personalize your copy if you order directly from my Website, www.kimberlyeinmo.com? (Ahem, please forgive the shameless plug.) Plan a pre-retreat shopping date with your buddies to hit your local quilt shop and choose your precut bundles of fabric goodies and any additional supplies, such as background fabric, thread, etc.

Here's a great idea: plan a strip swap or exchange toward the end of the retreat. Share the leftover strips and scraps from your quilts with each other and make a Bricks quilt (page 88). This will be a fun souvenir of your weekend retreat together and a great way to use up all those scraps!

K-I-S-S

Remember the old acronym again…. "Keep it simple, sweetie!" Planning is good, but don't knock yourself out trying to prepare to the "nth" degree! Your friends are coming to enjoy a great weekend with you stitching and playing with those wonderful fabric precut bundles; true friends don't really care if your house is spotless. Sure, it's nice to welcome guests to a tidy house and certainly you'll want to put clean sheets on the beds, but washing your windows or cleaning out closets before they arrive is just not necessary. Prepare, but don't wear yourself out before the fun starts. Save the housecleaning for after the retreat. (Or better yet, hire a one-time cleaning service.)

Fun with Friends

Just do it

Don't just *think* about hosting this fun event; get on the phone or e-mail and invite your friends! If you over-analyze the retreat, which is really just a grown-up girl's weekend slumber party, you'll never actually get around to hosting it and you'll miss out on loads of fun. Invite now, prepare later.

Enlist some help

You may not have to look beyond your own back yard for enlisted troops. Your kids may be willing to pitch in and help you prepare and play host in exchange for some extra video game time or a special trip to the movie theater complete with popcorn and soda. If you have friends who are not quilters, offer to trade services in exchange for them helping you to host your retreat. For example, if a neighbor is a terrific cook but not a quilter, invite her to "cater" your retreat. (You provide the food, she provides the preparation.) In exchange, offer to babysit for her children so she and her husband can go away on another weekend, or even promise to make her a quilt! If you have a teenage son, tell her you'll send him to mow her grass once a week for a month if she'll fix and serve the Friday night BBQ for you. You can always bribe junior with a prepaid iTunes gift card. Be creative. Barter.

Space, the not-so-final frontier

I'm referring to the space to hold your retreat, not outer space. If you want to host a Jelly Roll Retreat but holding it in your own home is just not an option, then look for alternative places such as a local church annex, school cafeteria, or even your local community center where there may be rooms you can use for little or no deposit or fee. Check with a local hotel as well for a conference room and hotel room package. In this economy, hotels may be eager to rent out space and rooms with a package deal. It might be cheaper than you think! This way, you can invite more buddies to join in the fun. You could open up your retreat to include your sewing group or even your entire guild. Keep an open mind and ask around for ideas and leads. Where there's a will, there's a way.

Eats

Will you serve all the food for the weekend or will it be pot luck? Consider slow cooker meals (I've provided great soup recipes on pages 55 and 87), deli trays, good old-fashioned take out (Chinese or pizza delivery is something everyone enjoys), or ask your husband to step in and help warm up a pre-made casserole and rolls. Don't forget munchies such as a veggie and/or fruit tray with dip, or even bagels and cream cheese.

There are plenty of snack items that don't have to blow your budget or anyone's diet such as popcorn, pretzels, cheese and crackers, or ever-the-crowd pleaser and my personal favorite: Kimberly's Nuts and Bolts! (See page 79 for the recipe.) You'll probably want to have at least one or two decadent desserts to indulge in, such as my delicious Best Brownies Ever (see page 74 for the ultimate recipe) or a few pieces of exquisite chocolate (Wilbur Buds, anyone?) to keep you stitching and giggling until the wee hours of the morning. Bottom line is, you're a quilter. You know what to do when it comes to food.

Goody bags

OK, this may be a little over the top, but give yourself a budget (no matter how small) and get creative! Everyone loves a goody bag and your friends will be delighted to find little bags of surprises at their sewing stations waiting just for them. It doesn't have to be much—a spool of thread, a Charm Pack, or even a package of needles and a piece of chocolate. But jazz it up and tie it with a bright bow or pretty ribbon. You might think about leaving a small basket of trial size toiletries in the guest bath just to make them feel a bit pampered, too.

Practical stuff

You need to consider details like having extra extension cords on hand and plenty of good lighting for everyone.

Be careful; you don't want a fire hazard with too many appliances plugged into an overloaded outlet. When in doubt, ask an electrical-savvy person to help set up the electronic configuration. There should be an appropriate number of irons plugged into different circuits, perhaps even some cutting stations set up, and trash cans strategically placed. If you have strong teenagers, ask them to help carry machines and chairs for the guests as they arrive, especially if there are stairs to navigate. Think safety first.

Fun!

Above all, have fun! This is your weekend to connect with friends and have a great time playing with precuts while doing what you love—making quilts! You'll have a ball laughing and sharing all weekend long, and you'll be amazed how much you really can accomplish while you're having fun.

Resources

I wish to sincerely thank the following companies for their support of products and services that helped to make this book possible. The fabric, batting, tools, and supplies featured or mentioned in this book are some of my personal favorites and can be purchased at your local quilt shop, sewing machine dealer, on the Internet, or by mail order. (Tell them Kimberly sent you!)

Moda Fabrics/United Notions
For generously providing all the fabric featured in the quilts in this book
13800 Hutton Drive
Dallas, TX 75234
Phone: 800-527-9447
E-mail: service@unitednotions.com
Web: www.unitednotions.com

Bernina of America
Sewing machines and accessories
3702 Prairie Lake Court
Aurora, IL 60504
Phone: 630-978-2500
E-mail: Jeanne@berninausa.com
Web: www.berninausa.com

American Quilter's Society
Publisher of top quality quilting books
P.O. Box 3290
Paducah, KY 42002-3290
Phone: 270-898-7903
E-mail: editor@aqsquilt.com
Web: www.americanquilter.com

The Simplicity Creative Group
Kimberly Einmo's:
  Easy Star & Geese Ruler
  Simpli-EZ Jelly Roll Ruler
  Easy Pineapple Log Cabin Ruler
  Easy Hearts Cutting Tool
and other quilting rulers, tools and notions
6050 Dana Way
Antioch TN 37013
Phone: 800-545-5740
E-mail: help@wrights.com
Web: www.ezquilt.com

The Electric Quilt Company
EQ6 and other quilting software
419 Gould Street, Suite 2
Bowling Green, OH 43402 -3047
Phone: 419-352-1134
Email: sales@electricquilt.com
Web: www.electricquilt.com

Rowenta USA
Irons and steamers
2199 Eden Road
Milville, NJ 08332
Phone: 800-ROWENTA
Web: www.rewentausa.com

Fairfield Processing Corp.
For generously providing all the batting used to make the quilts in this book
P.O. Box 1157
Danbury, CT 06813-1157
Phone: 800-980-8000
E-mail: tracyw@poly-fil.com
Web: www.poly-fil.com

YLI Threads
Variegated silk and other specialty threads used to make the quilts featured in this book
1439 Dave Lyle Blvd.
Rock Hill, SC 29730
Phone: 800-296-8139
E-mail:yligarrison@comporium.net
Web: www.ylicorp.com

Prym Consumer USA, Inc.
Omnigrid rulers and cutting mats
P.O. Box 5028
Spartanburg, SC 29304
Web: www.dritz.com

Olfa-North America
Rotary cutters
5500 N. Pearl Street, Suite 400
Rosemont, IL 60018
800-962-OLFA
Web: www.olfa.com

Sulky of America
Thread, stabilizers
P.O. Box 494129
Port Charlotte, FL 33949-4129
Phone: 800-874-4115
E-mail: infor@sulky.com
Web: www.sulky.com

Clover Needlecraft, Inc.
Sewing and quilting notions and tools
13438 Alondra Blvd.
Cerritos, CA 90703
E-mail: cni@clover-usa.com
Web: www.clover-usa.com

Schmetz
Sewing machine needles
9960 NW 116 Way, Suite 3
Medley, FL 33178
Web: www.schmetz.com

Jillily Studio Needle Arts
Appliqué glue
11626 Sunset Hills Dr.
Highland, UT 84003
Phone: 801-234-9884
E-mail: jill@jillilystudio.com
Web: www jillilystudio.com

Longarm Machine Quilting Services
In the USA:
Carolyn Archer
Ohio Star Quilting, Inc.
2895 Wilmington Road
Lebanon, OH 45036
Phone: 513-933-9008

In Europe:
Birgit Schüller
Creative BiTS
Schachtstrasse5
66292 Riegelsberg, Germany
Phone: +49 (6806) 920 447
E-mail: birgit.schuller@creativebits.biz
Web: www.creativebits.biz

Photography
Charlie Badalati Photography
E-mail: cb-photography@badalati.com
Web: www.badalati.com

About the Author

Kimberly Einmo is an author, designer, judge, and international quilting instructor. While living abroad, she designed a series of original quilts, many of which are featured in her first book, *Quilt a Travel Souvenir,* published by the American Quilter's Society. These stunning quilts capture the beauty and essence of the many different countries and exciting cities she visited in Europe.

Kimberly's articles and original quilts have appeared in a wide variety of publications including *McCall's Quilting* and *McCall's Quick Quilts* magazines, *American Quilter* magazine, *Quilter's Home* magazine, *Japanese Patchwork Tsushin* magazine, and *Irish Quilting* magazine. She has developed a line of innovative and exciting tools – including the brand new Simpli-EZ Jelly Roll Ruler, EZ Star & Geese Ruler, Easy Hearts Cut Tool, and EZ Pineapple Log Cabin Ruler – which are manufactured and distributed by the Simplicity Creative Group. She has also designed a popular and highly successful series of Mystery Quilts, which are in high demand by students everywhere.

Acclaimed both nationally and internationally, Kimberly has appeared as a repeat guest on the PBS series *America Quilts Creatively*. She has served as a full-time faculty member at the AQS Quilt Shows in both Paducah, Kentucky, and Des Moines, Iowa; as a judge, featured speaker, and instructor for many consecutive years at the Quilters' Heritage Celebration in Lancaster, Pennsylvania; at various Original Sewing & Quilt Expo events throughout the US; and she was the only instructor invited to represent the United States at the Annual Prague Patchwork Meeting in the Czech Republic in 2008. She'll be returning to teach in Prague in 2010. Kimberly has taught classes on several quilting cruises including destinations to the Caribbean, Mexico, and Alaska, with many more international appearances and quilt cruises scheduled through 2011.

Kimberly and Divot

Photo by Charlie Badalati

Kimberly was chosen to join the elite group of American Sewing Professionals who represent the Bernina Company throughout the US and abroad. She has also represented Pfaff as one of the VSM Sewing Stars since 2005. She truly enjoys sharing her passion for quilting and sewing with people everywhere, and is currently at work on her third book and designing a signature series of quilting patterns, notions, and tools for the Simplicity Creative Group.

Kimberly has been married for more than twenty years to her best friend, Kent, a retired U.S. Air Force officer, and they have two exceptional sons, Joshua and Andrew. To complete their household, they have one pampered pooch, Divot, and two cats, Tuffy and Poppy, who serve as Kimberly's "quality control managers" while she works.

For today's quilter ...
inspiration and creativity from

AQS Publishing

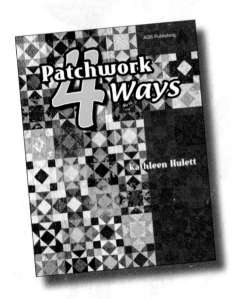

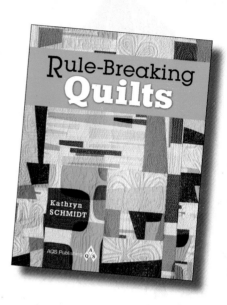

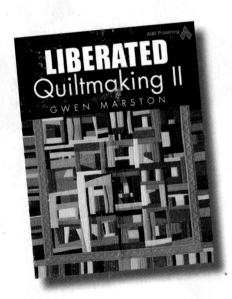

Look for these books nationally.
Call or Visit our Web site:

1-800-626-5420
www.AmericanQuilter.com